HOW LOSERS WIN

HOW LOSERS WIN

What No One Teaches You in School about
How to be Socially and Economically Free

Larry Gunter

CONTENTS

CHAPTER 1:

"Losers"

"Part of me suspects that I'm a loser, and the other part of me thinks I'm God Almighty."

- *John Lennon*

Loser What? Loser Who?

I wrote this book for each and every single one of you losers. I just know that there are a lot of you out there. I can feel you in my bones. I can see you in my minds' eye just going about your lives maybe not even fully aware that you are losers. Although I must say that most losers whom I have either come in contact with or read about are well aware that they are in fact losers. Some of you I'm sure have tried many times over to lose your loser status only to find that it is a lost cause. Another group of you losers doesn't even seem to be losers to the rest of the world. You are in hiding. You just can't seem to hide from yourself. What all of you losers have in common is your burning desire to not necessarily be a winner, but to no longer be a loser (More on this later). That goal, that ambition, that never-ending quest is all-consuming for you. You constantly ask yourself a series of questions like; why am I a loser? How do I not be one? What do I have to do? Where do I have to go? Whom do I have to meet? What sacrifices do I have to make, and on and on? Of course, you don't use the term loser when you confront yourself with these questions. By now you're probably on the verge of angrily tossing this book or reading device away. I must have some nerve to call you, who I do not know, a loser, right? Yes, the word loser is not a good word in our society. No one with a sane mind, sets out in the world to become a loser. Well, let me tell you here and now that the word loser in the context of this book is a good word. As the author of this book, I am proclaiming that as a fact. I would like for you, whether you are a loser yourself or are reading this on the behalf of your loser friend or family member, to keep an open mind. I promise that in these coming pages I will provide a clear and concise explanation to you of what a loser is and why being a loser can be a very good thing. I promise that by the end of this book, you will be equipped with the knowledge and understanding of how to be a loser that wins! Oxymoron as it may seem, in order for you to become the loser who wins that you are destined to be, I must first make it crystal clear just what a loser is. In order to do that, we must begin with what a loser is not. We must figure out and understand just what a winner is, and we will do just that in the next section. Oh! But before diving in, I must share one last tidbit of vital information with you. I, as the author of this book and instigator of several other perceivably outlandish entrepreneurial endeavors proudly shout from the top of my lungs, in text, this one simple fact; I AM A LOSER TOO!!!

Society Decides

Simply put a "winner" is no more than a social construct. Further, our society today has a totally different view of what a winner is than any society, say, 1,000 years ago considered a winner to be. I'm getting ahead of myself. Let's take a step back for a moment and define just what a society is. I mean if it is a society that determines what winners are, it is important to examine just what a society is. Let's look at the definition for our answer.

Society: the aggregate of people living together in a more or less ordered community.

Ok, so the keyword here is ordered. I think you all would agree that the opposite of order is random. So a simplified argument, for the basis of this discussion, of what society does can very well be that it prevents randomness by creating order. One might say it creates consensus. Our next question must be, "What is society creating order or consensus of?", right? Well looking back at the definition, it creates order or consensus within a community. A community itself is not a tangible thing. Therefore, what it essentially does is create order or consensus of the ideals that the members of the community hold in regards to how they will interact with each other. Acceptable behavior and unacceptable behavior is determined. It is then up to the members of the society to decide whether they will engage in favorable or unfavorable actions. The society will, to some degree, react to the behaviors of its members in accordance with the orderly norms that have been developed by the consensus of its members. The reactions to the members, as well as the degree of said actions, are also determined by the idealistic norms of the society. To illustrate this, imagine what would happen at the next wedding you attend if a large group in attendance began spitting on the bride and groom as they made their way down the aisle together. I would imagine that an all-out brawl wouldn't be too far of a reach.

Spitting on brides in their beautiful, oftentimes very expensive dresses on their special day is not acceptable behavior in our culture. In Greek culture, however, this was actually a thing. Spitting on brides was considered to be good luck and would ward off the devil. How do you suppose an employer would react to a phone call from an employee who states that they were going to miss a full day of work in order to have sex with their spouse? Umm, again I would say that there would be a pretty severe reaction to such an instance. Well, in Russian culture, they have implemented a holiday for getting it on. On the account of lowering populations, Russia assigned September 12th as its national day of conception. The Russian government is said to even give away prizes to new parents who in turn deliver exactly 9 months later. Other examples of what we would consider extremes in other cultures include: in Denmark they consider cemeteries to be great places to hang out socially, loud slurping when eating in Japan indicates that the food is tasty, and some cultures find pointing with your index finger or using your left hand to greet or eat to be highly offensive. If you find these cultural differences to be interesting be sure to search further online as I'm sure to have only scratched the surface.

Society influences the behavior of its members by developing customs and enforcing these customs by how it reacts to its members who display either affirming or negating behavior. Generally speaking, if a member engages in behavior that society advocates, the other members of the society will in consensus look up to the member. In turn, if a member engages in behavior that society frowns on, the other members of the society will in consensus look down at the member. Let's remember, we are interested in defining what a winner is. In order to find out specifically what a winner is, in our society, we must look at how the people in our communities behave when its members take various actions. For the sake of this book, we will be zeroing in on socioeconomic behavior. I will be ignoring behaviors in regards to performances like sporting events or market trends and behaviors such as those within stock markets, firms, or organizations. The focus will be solely on the socio-economic conditions of society.

A good strategy to identify what is acceptable and favorable behavior in society is to observe what its members convey to their children. People usually want the best that society has to offer for their children. In other words, they want their children to become winners once they become adults. Given this premise, just what is it that children in our society are told by adults with a positive interest in them being socially and economically successful in life? The answer is an obvious one. Children in our society are taught first and foremost to follow the rules of the law to ensure that they don't end up on the bad side of the judicial system. Children are also instructed on how important it is for them to get a quality education. Finally, children are encouraged to find a prestigious corporation that will employ them. That's it! We have achieved our goal. It's as simple as that. We now know what being a winner is in our society. If you stay clear of unlawful behavior, get a good education, and find yourself an opportunity to become an employee with a good company, then according to our society, you are a winner. Our children are told that by following these instructions, they will reap the rewards that our society has to offer, whether it be social recognition or financial gain.

Now that we have determined what a winner is, it is imperative that I now make an important distinction. Conventional thought would have us automatically draw a relationship between winners and losers. We would conclude that they are opposites. However, for the purpose of this book and the concepts contained here, I would ask you to refrain from doing so. If you are not a winner according to the definition that has just been established, that does not mean that you are in fact a loser. It may simply mean that you have not achieved the level of accomplishment that society requires for you to be a winner. Of course, there are varying degrees of success and what would be considered enough to be considered a winner by societies' standards. For the purpose of this book, we will not go beyond generalizations. It is also important to keep in mind that if you are in fact a loser, according to what definitive standards will soon be unearthed in the following pages, it does not mean that you are automatically exempt from being one of societies' winners. In this book, the terms winner and loser are not mutually exclusive. The purpose of this book is to help losers win. That fact does not implicate that being a winner is bad or negative. Focusing on losers, my aim is to refrain from presenting an opinion about those in society who choose to take the winners' path. Now with that piece of red tape taken care of and considering that we have a clear and concise idea of what winners are, it's time to begin the work of identifying what makes a loser, a loser. I will start by introducing you to some well-known losers who in some form or fashion managed to win.

When Win!?

So let's consider some real-life examples of losers who found their way in life and figured out a way to win. In order to make things a bit more interesting, we will be focusing primarily on people who became very wealthy despite their loser status. Millionaire status is not necessary for a loser to win. Success in life, from the vantage point of the loser, is all that is required. Yes, success is highly subjective, but we love rags to riches stories for a reason. They provide more bang for the buck. I want to show you all that the sky is the limit when it comes to winning. These examples of losers, some of which I'm sure you've heard of, truly display what each and every one of you is capable of.

I will be presenting this list of high achieving winning losers in 4 distinct categories. They are the "I Quitters", the "College Dropouts", the "Skippers", and the "Felons". This prestigious list, even if subconsciously, will begin to reveal the characteristics as well as the circumstances that define the term loser as it relates to this book. Without further ado, let's begin with the "I Quitters".

The I Quitters

Shep Murray & Ian Murray

Years ago, 27-year-old Shep Murray worked for a New York City based marketing and communications company as an advertising executive. At the same time, his 23-year-old brother Ian, was in public relations and worked at a small firm in Manhattan. Reverting back to our definition of winners, I would say that both brothers fit the description nicely. Both men still relatively young, had plenty of time to improve their lots even further by either moving up in the firms they worked or accepting positions with other companies. However, equipped with no more than an idea to start their own business, they both quit their jobs on the same day after one of them was told during a performance evaluation to "think inside the box." Their idea was to sell ties. Yep, selling ties was the big idea they confessed to everyone who asked why they had quit their jobs and wondered how they were going to make their livings moving forward. Needless to say, the 2 brothers did not receive very much support for their decision to quit their jobs. People constantly talked down to them and wondered how they could give up the career success they had achieved. Shep even admits that his girlfriend (now wife) was not happy about the decision. Yet they persevered. Their little selling ties idea has become Vineyard Vines, a company with 91 stores across the country. In 2016, Vineyard Vines was worth $1 billion dollars. These brothers quit their prestigious jobs and lost their status as winners in society. It all worked out in the end for the Murrays though. These losers ended up winning big! Here are other losers who, just like Shep and Ian, made the decision to abandon their achieved winner status and ultimately became successful by other means.

Paul English

Paul left his job at a venture capitalist firm to partner with another entrepreneur. Together they formed the travel website Kayak. Today Paul's net worth is $120 million dollars.

Andy Schamisso

Andy quit his job and his 13-year career in public relations to start a business selling tea using his wife's recipe. Fast forward 10 years or so from the time he quit and this once winner became a loser who won big. His company Inko's White Tea was reporting annual sales of around $3 million dollars.

Dana Sinkler and Alex Dzieduszycki

Dana and Alex had prestigious careers working in a restaurant for star chef Jean-Georges Vongerichten. Then they decided that being winners was not for them. They quit in order to start their own catering business. After experimenting with different recipes, they ended up creating an innovative veggie chip that was a huge success. They called them Terra Chips and ended up getting them into stores. After everything was said and done, Dana and Alex's business was a part of a bundle deal of companies that ended up selling for $80 million dollars. Terra Chips alone were said to have had $23 million in annual sales the year of the sale.

Adam Lowry and Eric Ryan

Adam was a climate scientist and his friend Eric worked in advertising. This was before both resigned from their jobs to create Method. Method would be an environmentally friendly cleaning product company that would later report gross revenue of over $100 million dollars. They too were winners who decided to become losers, and they won big.

The College Dropouts

Larry Ellison

In 1944, Larry was born to an unwed mother in New York City. At the tender age of 9 months, he contracted pneumonia and was given to his mothers' aunt and uncle for adoption. He wouldn't see his biological mother again until he was 48 years old. He ended up growing up in a middle-class neighborhood in Chicago with his adoptive parents. Larry attended college at the University of Illinois at Urbana-Champaign but withdrew after his second year when his adoptive mother died. Apparently still determined to be a winner, he attended the University of Chicago for a single term. Larry would not return back to college but would enter the workforce where he further developed his computer and programming skills. It wouldn't be long before he formed Oracle. The company that led him to be listed by Forbes as one of the richest men in the world. Larry would continue to work in the tech world ultimately becoming a tech legend. Despite such humble beginnings, Larry Ellison still managed to end up being on the fast track to being a winner in society. However, he abandoned his efforts in college derailing his prospects. It all worked out fine in the end.

As of 2017, this loser was estimated by Forbes to be the 4th richest person in tech. In June of 2018, his net worth was reported at about $54.5 billion dollars. Not too bad for a loser huh? Are you catching on to the trends yet? Let's continue with a few other losers who, like Larry, were on their way to becoming winners but decided to drop out of college in order to pursue a different path.

Ellen Degeneres

You know this one right? Ellen is a huge success in the entertainment world. Did you know that after only 1 semester of college, she dropped out and worked odd jobs while pursuing her career in comedy? Well, it wasn't long before she got her big break and it all became worth it. Some sources report that her current net worth is a whopping $450 million dollars. Ellen Degeneres is clearly a loser who has done very well for herself. She has won big!

Russell Simmons

Here is another example of a loser becoming wildly successful in the entertainment arena. Russell Simmons, who dropped out of the City College of New York in Harlem, has to be mentioned as one of the pioneers responsible for making hip hop music the huge success it has become. As one of the co-founders of the record label Def Jam, along with other endeavors, he created quite a bit of bank for himself. Russell Simmons reportedly has a current net worth of approximately $340 million dollars.

Steve Jobs

At the time of his death, Steve Jobs had a reported net worth of approximately $10.2 billion dollars. He spent only one semester in college on the winners' path. This loser did pretty well for himself.

Bill Gates and Paul Allen

These losers spent a year or so in college before dropping out to start this tiny little company we now know as Microsoft. Paul Allen has a reported net worth of around $20 billion while Bill Gates is at a whopping $102 billion dollars! Wow! It is a huge understatement to say that these two losers won big.

The Skippers

Richard Branson

Richard was not a very good candidate for becoming a winner from very early on in life. He managed to stay clear of the law, but he had dyslexia and struggled with school. On his last day of school, one of his teachers told him that his life would end of taking one of two paths. He said Richard would either be in prison or become a millionaire. This teacher was correct to leave out a third option of him becoming a winner. He was confident that Richard would skip college altogether, and he was right. Richard did take early to entrepreneurship though. I'm sure this had much to do with his family's support of his endeavors. His mother was even a bit of an entrepreneur herself. After several failed attempts, Richard launched his first successful business, a magazine called *Student,* when he was only 16 years old. Very soon after, he launched his own record store where he found a competitive advantage over his competitors. With 2 successful entrepreneurial endeavors under his belt, Richard would not be done. He was just getting started in fact. Richard Branson would go on to launch over 400 companies under his parent company Virgin Group. He was not successful academically in grade school on the account of his learning disability and ended up abandoning college altogether. He was clearly not interested in becoming one of society's winners as he opted to pursue various entrepreneurial endeavors. It paid off big for Sir Richard Branson who has a net worth today of around $4.1 billion dollars. Way to go, sir! Now let's briefly look at other winning losers who skipped college altogether, completely abandoning their prospects of becoming one of society's winners.

Gisele Bundchen

Gisele decided to abandon any pursuits of becoming a winner when she, at the tender age of 14, decided to launch her modeling career. She was 16 when she had her first break in New York City. It wouldn't be long before this loser was modeling for some of the most prestigious brands in the business including Dolce & Gabbana, Ralph Lauren, and Versace. She would go on to appear on more than 1,200 magazine covers around the world. Her net worth currently hovers around the $400 million dollar mark. She won big!

David H. Murdock

With a net worth of about $1.9 billion dollars, you would never think that David H. Murdock dropped out of high school in the 9th grade. College and thus the path to being a winner was not in the cards for him. He instead enlisted in the United States Army during World War II and became homeless after the war. He eventually landed on his feet finding opportunities in small businesses and real estate endeavors which would lead to more holdings in various other companies. This loser found a way to win big despite dropping out of high school and even being homeless for a spell.

Ray Kroc

Ray Kroc is the man responsible for bringing us the super restaurant brand McDonalds. He never went to college and had to work a variety of jobs during the Great Depression to make ends meet. His ambition would ultimately lead him to pursue a vision he had for a restaurant that he himself did not originally start. It was a vision that would eventually put McDonald's restaurants on virtually every city corner around the world. This loser didn't do too bad for himself either with a net worth equivalent to $1.4 billion dollars in today's money at the time of his death.

Walt Disney

Where is it that you want to go when you have won the Super Bowl, World Series, or NBA Championship? You want to go to Disney World of course! Walt Disney's works are known by households around the world which is saying a lot for someone who decided that higher education was a nay for him. As an entrepreneur, animator, voice actor, and film producer, Walt laid the groundwork for a whopping current net worth of $130 billion dollars for the company Disney alone.

The Felons

Frederick Hutson

Growing up in Brooklyn, New York with his single mother and three siblings, Frederick could not have guessed the twists and turns he would experience in his life. He would eventually move to Florida in his teens and serve in the United States Air Force. He would run several businesses there. At the age of 19, he had a window tinting business where he made about $50,000. He would be eventually honorably discharged from the Air Force on the account of downsizing. He then decided to use his entrepreneurial skills for illegal activities. He began to transport marijuana through parcel companies. He was very successful financially netting approximately a half a million dollars a year. However, as is often the case with illegal activities, his luck ran out. The DEA arrested him at the age of 23 and he was sent to prison. Frederick ended up serving 51 months before being released to a half-way house. While serving his time in prison, he being the witty entrepreneur he was, saw a problem that he felt he could solve. He found it difficult for inmates to communicate with their family and friends that were outside of the institution. This led him to found the company Pigeonly once he was released. Pigeonly makes it easier for incarcerated individuals to find people and information by providing access to its massive database. Pigeonly also has a phone component that is similar to Google Voice and Skype that does the work of finding the cheapest connection solutions to the people that inmates seek to talk to. The company was a huge success! As of 2014, Pigeonly was reported to be a $3 million dollar business. This loser ended up winning even after breaking the very first lesson in becoming a winner in society. He got into trouble with the law and served over 4 years in prison. Let's look at a couple of other losers who got into trouble, yet found a way to win!

Frank Abagnale

Frank also served around 4 years in prison. He decided to conduct himself as a con man, check forger, and imposter early in his life. After serving his time, he changed his life around and eventually began working for the federal government along with starting his own financial fraud consultancy company. His current net worth is about $10 million dollars!

Coss Marte

This 3-time felon and former drug kingpin grew up in Manhattan's Lower East Side in New York and was no stranger to drugs, violence, and poverty. Idolizing the drug dealers, he was introduced to the lifestyle early on. He became very successful at it making over $2 million a year at the age of 19. Four years later he would be caught and sentenced to 7 years in prison. In prison and out of shape, he became concerned about his health and began working out. He ended up losing 70 pounds in just 6 months. After being released from prison, ultimately serving 10 years, he decided to capitalize on his exercise program he developed in prison and started Coss Athletics. His new company became very successful. In 2016 he had about 400 clients and made approximately $10,000 per month. Despite being exiled from society for 10 years of his life, this loser still managed to win big!

The common thread in all of these losers is undeniably that they ended up making choices that kept them from either keeping or attaining winner status. The "I Quitters" became winners by society's standards and choose to walk away from it all. The "College Dropouts" were working towards obtaining their winner status when they decided to drop out of school and do their own thing. The "Skippers" did not even bother to get on the boat towards "Winnersville". Finally, the "Felons" broke arguably the most important rule in the pursuit of becoming a winner by getting into trouble with the law and going to prison. Reflecting on these examples of losers, the main takeaway is that any loser no matter the circumstance can end up winning. You may have already developed a good intuitive idea of what a loser is after these examples. However, I caution you that the true definition of a loser is not so black and white. We will examine the concept of winning as a loser a little further in the next section.

MORE LUCK WITH MY WINNING PLEASE!!!

A simple Google search online will provide one with many sources that make the same claim. Simply put, the more education you get the higher your income will be. It goes as follows, the Doctorate grad makes more than the grad with the Masters, who makes more than the 4 year undergrad, who makes more than the 2 year associate grad, who triumphs the high school grad, who finally makes more than the poor souls who don't manage to even graduate from high school. I am sure there is substantial validity to these claims. People who are much smarter than I work on this stuff. I'm sure they have their many resources as well as surveys and questionnaires or what have you. Again, I don't doubt, nor do I argue against these claims. So let's just, here and now, agree that they are true. The more education you receive, the more money you will make is a statistical fact in regards to society's members as a whole. If you don't graduate high school or you end up in prison, you will most likely struggle to make it socioeconomically in our society. Statistically speaking, where you fall on the hierarchy of your educational endeavors will determine where you land in life in relation to where others in society have landed who have more or less education than you do. Again, prison time is like introducing a negative number to the comparison as it sets one way back behind the herd socioeconomically right? Well, if this is the case, what is needed for someone who is not a winner to succeed in life? As my examples clearly state, sometimes people are successful who don't follow the winners' path. Their success goes against everything that our society advocates for and that the statistics clearly layout before us. You know, those statistics and economic studies that very smart people present for us all to see. The more education you are able to acquire the more money you will make in your lifetime and thus the better off you are socioeconomically, right? Well, for those that don't realize substantial education, yet are able to win big at times making millions of dollars, there can only be one explanation. It must be luck. They are at the right place at the right time, or just happen to stumble across a one in a lifetime opportunity at a time where they were prepared to take advantage of it. They were lucky enough to live in a region where they had access to a major player in a big game. Yes, that must be it. Luck! Something that there is only a small amount of in the world and only a few people are able to capitalize on enough to win. Luck is the answer, right? Umm, nope!

There are a few lucky people out in the world who win big on the account of luck of circumstance. However, none of the winners I mentioned fit the bill. In fact, most of the losers who make it big wish that they had luck on their sides. I'm sure it seemed like the opposite of luck was what they were experiencing when they were in the trenches. Society is not very kind to those who are not on the winners' path. Not saying that is good or bad, it just is what it is. In order for a logical system to work, it has to make sense. If society values its winners then it must value the behavior that winners embark on. In turn, if it values the way that winners behave then it systematically must devalue the behavior of those who do not behave like winners. If you go to prison, you have a record that is socially and economically frowned on. If you don't graduate high school, employers are not going to be too kind to you when you seek to work in their establishments. On the social side of things, we may not even realize it but we want to associate with people who behave like winners. This means we hold it against people who don't. How would you feel if your beloved son or daughter brought home a high school dropout? What about if you found out your new next-door neighbors had just been released from prison after serving 10 years? How about if your fiancée without warning suddenly quit their promising job at a prestigious law firm? Generally speaking, we do not behave favorably towards those that make decisions or on the account of circumstances go against what our society considers winners. This explains the phenomenon of how many wealthy people receive things free such as meals at restaurants. At the same time, a homeless person may be turned away from the restaurant even when attempting to pay. This is why the luck argument does not hold water here. The losers who win have to contend with the consequences of their actions to abandon what society values. This means that their opportunities are most likely diminished instead of enhanced.

So what is it then? What does it take? How can it be explained that despite what the statistics and the experts say about the positive correlation between education and salary, some losers still manage to win? Some of them even win big. How is it that I can write a book claiming to have the answers to how any loser can win? The answer to these very important questions highlights an essential component in our efforts to identify what a loser truly is. I mentioned earlier that all of you losers reading this book have a similar characteristic. That is a burning desire to not necessarily be a winner but to win. That burning desire is a significant part of what makes a loser, a loser. It has nothing to do with where you are currently in life nor where you have been. It can be with you for as long as you can remember or be newly acquired. This unshakable burning desire is what drove every single one of the losers in my examples to succeed. It caused many of them to quit their jobs or school. It forced them to face societal rejections as they moved forward with their visions. No one, except maybe sociopaths, actually enjoy being outcasts of society. Losers choose a different path, but if they had it their way they would have people cheer them on. It would be great if others would join in with them. I'm sure it would've made the aforementioned winning losers' struggles to succeed a lot easier if that were the case. If only they had luck and a society which believed in them on their sides. I assure you they did not and neither will you.

It takes a certain type of person to endure these challenges. Everyone in society does not fit neatly into either winner or loser camps. There are plenty of those who strive to be winners but for whatever reason fall short. These individuals have no desire to be losers and that is perfectly fine. There are also plenty of individuals that go to prison, don't finish high school, drop out of college, or quit their jobs with prestigious firms who are not losers. As I noted at the beginning of this book there are also losers who are in hiding. As far as society is concerned they are winners or striving to become winners. They can be found in college classrooms as well as in business boardrooms. They vary from having little income to having millionaire status. What makes them different, and thus losers is that they have that burning desire for something different that they cannot escape. Society appears to do its job very well in that there are more winners and aspiring winners than there are losers walking around. This is a good thing. Society needs order and consensus to function properly. However, it also needs some of its members to go against the grain. This is where losers shine! They have that unshakable burning desire to not just work on innovative things but to live innovative lives. They don't rely on luck to succeed. In fact, if they win, they all too often have to do so despite society and its members turning their backs on them. Losers are a special breed! They possess innate qualities that enable them to combine their fiery ambitions, pit them against seemingly overwhelming odds, and come out on top after everything is said and done. If the question is... "How does a loser win?" or "How does a loser win big?", such as was the case with the examples above. The answer is quite simple. A loser wins because they are in fact losers. It's in their DNA. If you are a loser, then it's in yours too!

LOO-WHO?-ZUH-HER

Putting it plainly, losers and winners are social constructs, but there is more to it than that. No one can just look at someone's actions or position in life and say definitively that they are a loser. There may be clues present in the losers' behavior that hint to whether or not they are. At the end of the day, the person must examine themselves. It doesn't matter where you currently are in your life. You could be in prison or the CEO of a Fortune 500 company. If you have a burning desire that you cannot shake to deviate from what society considers winner behavior and you desperately need to embark on your own path of innovation and exploration, then you are a loser. It is just that simple. You may have a burning desire to deviate from your job or your school so that you can land a job with another firm or go to another school. This does not qualify you as a loser. Further, you may want to deviate from work or school, but you don't have a desire to do anything innovative with your life. If this is you, then guess what? You are not a loser either. You may even have a desire to do something innovative, but don't have that burning desire to deviate from your job or school. This implies that you aren't prepared to commit to your ambitions and goals. What you have is most likely a desire to pursue a hobby or an intriguing interest. In the end, you will probably fall short and resort back to what makes you comfortable. A true loser finds it very uncomfortable what many of those who aren't losers find comfortable, most notably being a winner.

Now that we have fully defined and examined what it means to be a loser, many of you may be wondering why I choose to use the word loser. I could've very easily picked another term to describe the above type of person right? Well, the simple answer is that the word loser is the most correct term in our society for what such a person is. We all know exactly what our winners are. Society defines them and their behavior very well. However, the type of person that I just described is not those things. Society will not accept them. They will be outcasts and in many regards considered to have lost at the game of life. It is from society's perspective that the term loser is used in this book. I do not consider someone who chooses to deviate from winner behavior to be someone who will most likely lose at life, but our society with its many players and systems does. If you fit the description outlined in the text above and you choose to act accordingly, society will begin to cast you out as one of its losers and it will treat you as such. Majority of the people and institutions in society will treat you as the loser it has pegged you to be. I am here to tell you that it's ok and that you should wear your loser status as a badge of honor. Be proud to be a loser. Remember, it is just a social construct after all. It only means that you will not be a winner as defined by society. If you are a true loser, you have probably already come to terms with that within yourself. The word loser should serve to remind you that you are explorative and innovative. It should remind you that there are many exciting twists and turns laying ahead of you. This is when you are in your comfort zone anyways so it's all good.

Personally, I am perfectly fine with accepting my status as a loser and all that it entails. As the final example of losers who won, let me briefly share my personal story with you. I am a 6-time college dropout. No misprint there. I have dropped out of 6 different higher learning institutions on 6 different occasions. The reason for my college dropout record has nothing at all to do with academics. I am and have always been a very capable student. If anything, my experience has been that things moved a bit too slow for me. I would always catch on to a topic and have to wait for my classmates to get it before instructors would move on to the next topic. So why would I fail at college, and why would I do it so many times is the question that must be looming in your minds at this point? Another quite simple answer here, the reason is that I am a loser and have been for a very long time. In all 6 attempts, the first of which was just over 20 years ago, all I could manage to muster up was a 2-year degree in business administration. That's it! Along the way, I registered to major in business, sociology, IT, project management, and audio production. Society would focus on my failure to complete higher education as a personal flaw. I definitely earned my loser classification. No matter how many times I failed over the years, I kept on signing back up for school. The reason I continued is that I needed to win. I did not yet know how or why I was unfit to be one of society's winners, but I had a burning desire to win. Interestingly, over the years, I had completed many other non-traditional things on my own. I bought a digital camera and taught myself photography. I became very good at graphic design. I taught myself how to write songs, record music, and mix and master audio. I very often wrote poetry, I taught myself the basics of computer programming. I created board games from scratch. I taught myself a bit on videography and video editing. I taught myself how to use Microsoft's Excel, where I would create analytical tools for various endeavors. I studied story structure and wrote movie screenplays and short stories. I developed many plans for business endeavors as well as nonprofit organizations, and I studied and coached youth basketball. The list goes on and on. I didn't know it at the time, but I was behaving just as a loser does. I was not someone who wanted to become a winner and was just incapable of doing so. This by no means explains my inability to complete my higher education. Perhaps in the absence of all the other endeavors, it may have. Instead what motivated me to keep enrolling in school as well as to embark on all the other activities and projects that I would do was that strong burning desire to win. Remember, this is one of the parts essential to someone who is a loser. The other part is the need to innovate in ones' life.

My biggest error was considering my desire to win the same as my desire to become a winner. This is a very important distinction. I have no trouble with motivation and desire when embarking on winning activities. On the other hand, I find it extremely difficult when attempting to sustain motivation and desire when embarking on behavior geared towards becoming a winner. If this is you, then that is a sure sign that you are a loser like me. I encourage you to embrace the loser inside of you. Feel good about it. Unfortunately for me, I was not given this advice. After the constant fluctuating behavior between working on becoming a winner and working to becoming a loser who wins, I was left feeling as though I was a failure. Society was not accepting me and it left me depressed and unsure of my own abilities. What was wrong with me I would ask as I would fail to complete assignment after assignment eventually leading to withdrawal from the universities I was attending.

This does not have to be you. If it has been, it doesn't have to be anymore. I have found my way and you can too. This book will help you get there! You may be a loser by society's standards, but you are not a failure! You are just as capable of achieving success and making people proud as any of society's winners are. Please understand that you are not alone. There are many losers out there in the world who are just like you. I am one of them and I managed to win. In the remainder of this book, my goal is to show you how you can win too. It is important that you win on your terms. In the next couple of chapters, we will look at just that. Realizing that you are a loser and not interested in going the winners' path is one thing, but finding your own individual path is another thing altogether. It may seem cut and dry, but there are lots of things present in society that can make this extremely difficult. The most important thing is to embrace who you truly are despite the external appeals present that provoke you to behave in ways that you are truly not. Be a loser! Get the T-shirt! Wear it as a badge of honor! This is the most important step in becoming a loser who wins!

CHAPTER 2

Pinocchio's Revolution

"The great revolution in the history of man, past, present, and future is the revolution of those determined to be free."

-John F. Kennedy

The American Dream

What is it that we all strive for? If you closed your eyes right now and imagined what your life would look like once you have made it, what would you see? In other words, what does the American Dream look like? You would see yourself completely financially and time free wouldn't you? You would probably find yourself lying on the world's best beaches, relaxing with friends and family in one of your large estates, or traveling the world experiencing all it is that life has to offer. Even though each of you would have different versions of what your American Dream looks like, each of them would share the same underlying theme. We see it in the movies we watch. It's in the magazine ads for the consumer products that we use. We see it in our social media feeds as people we know post snapshots of the lives they wish they could live all the time. It is branded in our minds that the American Dream is all of that and we need to get some, Right? Let's go back to your imagined view of your American Dream. How do you look in it? Are you in good health?

How about the people in your life there to experience it all with you? How do they look? Is everyone there? Are they all in good health? The vision that you are probably having of your American Dream is taking place in present time. We don't usually dream of living our paradise once we've reached senior citizen status. If you are presently a senior then the vision of your dreams aren't taking place 10-15 years from now. We may think that we can only actually achieve it in the future, but I'm talking about our dreams here. We want it all and we want it now, right?

All of you would no doubt love to be living your version of the American Dream. How many of you truly think that you can obtain it though? Is it something that we really strive for each and every day or is it more like a carrot occasionally dangling in our faces that provides us with a "one day I'll make it" hope of success? If we really think of it, we don't hold these paradise versions of the American Dream too close to our day to day lives. We may want and wish that for ourselves but often times we consider those who have achieved American Dream status to be of a special elite or even a lucky few. Let's take a moment to think about who these people are. I'm referring to the wealthiest people in our society. Here is a list of the current top 15 wealthiest Americans and the sources of their wealth as of February 2019 from the Bloomberg Billionaires Index.

1.	Jeff Bezos	$131.4 billion	Amazon.com
2.	Bill Gates	$96.4 billion	Microsoft...
3.	Warren Buffet	$82.6 billion	Berkshire
4.	Larry Ellison	$62.4 billion	Oracle
5.	Mark Zuckerberg	$62.1 billion	Facebook
6.	Larry Page	$60 billion	Google
7.	Charles Koch	$50.4 billion	Koch Industries
8.	David Koch	$50.4 billion	Koch Industries
9.	Sergey Brin	$49.9 billion	Alphabet
10.	Michael Bloomberg	$48.7 billion	Bloomberg L.P.
11.	Jim Walton	$44.6 billion	Walmart
12.	S. Robson Walton	$44.3 billion	Walmart
13.	Alice Walton	$44.4 billion	Walmart
14.	Steve Ballmer	$41.2 billion	Microsoft...
15.	Sheldon Adelson	$35.1 billion	Las Vegas Sands

Each of these people listed has more than enough money to live the American Dream that you envision. Yet, I do realize that the amount of wealth that they possess may not be necessary to live your vision. However, it is a good practice to look at those ablest to realize the desired outcome and examine their circumstance when evaluating ones' own actions. The obvious common theme here is that they all own businesses. Therefore, it is not a huge stretch to conclude that a proven way to realize your American Dream would be to own businesses (We will talk quite a bit more about this later). Yet, how many of you actually own businesses outright or through stock?

My point is simple. We usually don't focus on the American Dream we have as a real possibility of how our lives will turn out. We flirt with the idea of grabbing that dangling carrot that lay before us but instead live our lives in pursuit of a lifestyle that we consider accessible.

Where do these images of our idealized lifestyles come from? A place where human ideas are manufactured of course. They come from our society. This isn't to say that a life lived on a beach resort would suck. Majority of us would probably consider such a lifestyle to be highly desired. What society does is bring order to the chaos. Instead of focusing on a large number of idealized American Dreams, it creates a common idea in each of our minds that we can all then strive for. Again, there is absolutely nothing wrong with this. I'd go so far as to say a healthy and properly functioning society should contain such social tools. This is how we are able to make sense of what is going on in our communities and in our individual lives. If we want to know how someone is doing socioeconomically, and we see them with fancy cars living on a beach, we instantly know. We can then make better decisions as to how we deal with people. Are we going to invest half of our savings with the guy who we always see hanging out at the corner store soliciting people as they walk by for spare change? Probably not.

Where we should take a deeper look at how our society is functioning has to do with upward mobility. Upward mobility is the capacity or facility for rising to a higher social or economic position. So, it is perfectly fine for society to define for us what higher socioeconomic statuses will look like, but what is not ok is for it to deny us a real chance at upward mobility. That dangling carrot that lay before us must be obtainable. After all, in America, you can become anything you want. This is the very place that people come from far and wide to get to. They want to take a bite of that old American Pie. There are very few places like the United States of America, where someone can go from being the poorest of us to among the richest within their lifetimes. Do you think this American Dream the U.S. is known for and constantly advertises is realistically obtainable? Do you think that if one of our society's members display hard work and determination that they can obtain this dream? I say that America is not fibbing when it tells us that we too can live our lives on a beach without a care in the world in regards to time or money. However, I will have to put an asterisk beside that answer. The reason being is that American society is blatantly misleading us.

There are many scholars and experts who examine upward mobility and the real chance people have to realize the dream lifestyle in many societies. We will be looking at the work of Professor Raj Chetty who, among others, has transformed our understanding of social mobility in America. I want to shed some light on what is really going on here. Off the gate, let's look at the chances of making it from the bottom 20% to the top 20% of the wealth in one's lifetime. The study considered the United States, United Kingdom, Denmark, and Canada. The consensus of thought is that people do not travel far and wide to go to Canada, Denmark, or the UK for the American Dream right? The American Dream can only be harnessed from right here in the great U.S. of A. This has to make us feel as though we are in the place to be. The power is in our hands and we can only pity people in the other countries who are less fortunate than us in regards to upward mobility. Well, not so fast. Let's look at the data.

PROBABILITY THAT A CHILD BORN TO PARENTS IN THE BOTTOM FIFTH OF INCOME DISTRIBUTION REACHES THE TOP FIFTH.

Canada	13.50%	
Denmark	11.70%	
United Kingdom	9.00%	
United States of America		7.5%

Wow! These findings are stunning right? According to these results, People living in Canada are nearly twice as likely to achieve the American Dream as People living in America are! To drive this misleading notion of the American Dream further, let's look at another category. How has American upward mobility performed over time? In other words, how have your chances of realizing the American Dream changed when compared to those of your parents or grandparents? Well, these findings are pretty astounding as well. In short, the last few decades have seen a very sharp decline in upward mobility. More specifically, the study examined Americans born in 1940 and found that the majority of them ended up better off than their parents. When they looked at those born 40 years later in 1980, it was a completely different story. Only half of these people ended up better off than their parents!

What this work by Professor Raj Chetty shows is that the American Dream that American society is known for isn't actually as accessible as it may seem. The work goes clearly points out that rates of upward mobility aren't just unimpressive, but are actually declining. The million-dollar questions are why? and what does it mean for losers like you and me? I mentioned that I was not in the camp of believing that America's Dream is a lie. I will go so far as to say that it can be relatively easily accessed. However, we are in fact being strongly misled by our society as to how one achieves the American Dream. American society flaunts its dream to its constituents like the golden ticket in Willy Wonka's Chocolate Factory. However, it doesn't exactly advocate for us to go about attempting to get this golden ticket in the most obvious way. As stated before, the most successful way to obtain the American Dream is by owning businesses. However, becoming an entrepreneur is not the type of behavior that society's winners display. Remember that Society says that if you want to become a winner you must stay out of trouble, get as much education as possible, and find you a job with a prestigious firm. Entrepreneurship is not how you become a winner, but it is apparently how you realize the American Dream. So why does American society flaunt its dream for us as a golden ticket in the Willy Wonka movie yet advocate a totally contradictory socioeconomic behavior altogether? I have a theory which I will present in the next section. The point here is that as Losers, the odds aren't totally stacked against us. The fact that we are not winners does not decrease our chances of realizing our version of the American Dream. It can actually be seen as increasing our chances if we consider the source of wealth from the wealthiest Americans as well as Americas' little secret considering just how obtainable upward mobility isn't.

The Matrix

I remember my first time seeing the Movie the Matrix. It completely blew my mind. I have always been a fan of science fiction and this movie really got me to thinking "what if?". If in fact, we were all plugged into some system that made our lives and the entire way that we lived them complete lies, I wanted to be Neo. Keanu Reeves' character was the chosen one after all. He was the only person in the movie who was able to be more powerful than this huge complex system by using nothing more than his mind. It didn't matter how physically fit he was, his IQ level, who he knew, or how much money he had. All that mattered was his ability to locate and maintain his true self at an extremely high level despite being plugged into this great system that was designed to control him. The Matrix, as it is referred to in this science fiction movie, was run by machines. Could it be possible that we have our own version of the matrix to deal with in our lives? Are there forces in our society that are designed to control the way we think and behave? I would say absolutely. A major difference is that these forces are not being controlled by machines. They are being created and controlled by people with agendas. This is no big conspiracy theory or anything like that. What I am actually referring to is common knowledge. Take a look around you. Virtually everything that we interact with has a brand attached to it. We can't even purchase an age-old natural resource such as water without making a decision as to whose water we will be purchasing. Looking for some new shoes to replace the worn out ones you have? Well, you will need to decide which brand to go with. What about your phone/portable computer system? You have to make a decision there as well. We are surrounded by brands at every turn. Oh, and it is not in these brands' best interest to just let the market decide on its own which products or services those in society will choose. They have to put forth the effort to persuade you to go with them instead of the other guy or gal, right? That's what we call capitalism in this country. By the way, the "They" I mentioned in regards to the brands are the people who are employed with the brand. Those in upper management who have been taxed with ensuring that their company makes financial gains year after year after year. They have to keep the stockholders happy you know. Failing to do so too often will virtually always result in a letter of resignation. Those in power positions no doubt throw large amounts of company money at this problem to make sure that doesn't happen. This is Corporate America. Thousands of big businesses using large amounts of money to get us to do something they desperately need us to do. What do they spend this money on you ask? Well, the obvious thing is advertising. One report in 2017 said that the Advertising industry was worth a whopping $1.2 Trillion dollars. That's a lot of money being spent to control... Oops, I meant to persuade us to buy products. No, I really did mean control us. Advertising is a huge industry, but it doesn't account for all that is being used to control us. What about our government. We have 3 separate bodies of power to ensure that we are being governed in a fair and just way, correct? Well, the congressional branch is the branch that is mostly connected to how we in society live. The people in Congress develop the rules that we live by. There is some huge controlling power there. We the people elect these individuals so we have the say-so over how we are governed, right? I say think again. Take a look at the major campaign contributions reported by our news sources being contributed by the same people who pay for advertising and tell me that they are paying large and small fortunes to help their favored candidate get elected because they just like the guy. I am not the first to say it, but our political system and thus our government has been compromised. What do these powerful corporations and the people behind them get in return for their major campaign contributions? I will let you ponder on that question yourself. It is an open-ended question that I can only hope you all will look into for yourselves. It might help change our voting practices and trends. In any event, the government controls us by mandating our behavior and our systems to abide by protocols that it puts in place. Moving on, we've considered advertising and government policies/laws as controlling mechanisms in our society and though there are many more, I will only mention one other here. Have you turned on the news or looked at your newsfeed lately? The news by definition is where we go to see how our society is doing. It is the way that we check our society's temperature so-to-speak. If we hear on the news, for example, that there is a rise in a threatening behavior from one group of people, then once consuming this information we in society will alter the way we behave according to this news. On the other hand, if the news reports that a certain group, system, firm, or institution is engaging in behavior that is welcomed, it will most likely change our perception and behavior towards the entities mentioned in a positive way. Again, let's look at who in in control. We oftentimes see the same corporations and major players either owning our news sources or heavily contributing to their content. They would do the last bit by pushing or pulling their advertising dollars to and from media outlets according to the programming that they present. I have always found it fascinating that our media and entertainment outlets use the term "programming" when referring to their content.

In the previous sections, we looked at the chances we losers have of obtaining the American Dream. We examined how American society from a big-picture perspective is misleading in how assessable upward mobility is. Being a winner in our society is all fine and well, but it probably isn't the path one should take if they want to realize the American Dream that they envision for themselves right now. Coming down from our birds-eye view, we surely don't live in a matrix system being controlled by machines. Well, at least there is no evidence of that. However, we are in a society that, just like the matrix, has players, institutions, firms, and organizations which are putting forth an enormous amount of money and effort to control our behavior. This is not a conspiracy theory. It is the reality of the way America's capitalistic system works. It is important that we, as losers, are aware of these powers and their agendas if we are to win. If you believe that knowledge is power, as I do, then you can easily see how power over your own mind and ideals in your day to day life is essential to you setting the course towards the win that you so desperately desire. Let's look at another concept that has been an effective tool those in power often use to control our behavior.

Us v/s Them

Did you know that there is a shortcut way to gain the favor

of people that you interact with in society? Even though this social phenomenon has been happening around me for my entire life, it took an unfortunate circumstance at work for me to see it. I was working as a new manager for a firm that provided a service to another firm. They were essentially our bosses. If we didn't provide the service to their customers adequately, they would come at us with questions and we needed to provide answers. Well, my predecessor at the management position did not do a very good job of keeping them (our client) happy. Having held a similar position before, I was brought in to make things right so the client wouldn't be lost. At around the same time I was hired as manager, our client created a new management position in order to resolve some internal challenges they were facing. I would be dealing directly with this new manager. After meeting him and seeing how he operated, it was not long at all before I realized that he wasn't very capable as a manager. I thought to myself it wouldn't be long before they realized that the guy wasn't very much help and got rid of him. I would have been right too, but the new manager knew the social shortcut I referenced and he used it to perfection. He knew that his company had been very unhappy with the service my company had provided prior to my arrival. With this information, his primary focus became to seek and find anything bad about the company I worked for. If he was unable to find anything, he was putting his efforts into making something up. He made sure that we continued to be the villains so that he did not have to be a hero or to even contribute. If there was a problem going on, it undoubtedly had to be on account of us. Despite not having any real arguments against us, as I had eventually fixed virtually all of the problems with our service, he created such a ruckus that he was still able spent the majority of his time coming up with rules and mandating how we did our jobs. The shortcut or social trick that he used was that he identified an enemy of his constituents and then over-exaggerated the significance or importance of this enemy. This trick may seem cynical and I don't advocate for or against using it. I am simply stating that it works. The people in the company he worked for could no longer see what it was that he was doing, or in this case, was not doing. All they could see was the issues that he was presenting and exaggerating to them. The reality of what was going on and more importantly in this example, the reality of his contribution or value was completely ignored. Everyone was focused on the problem. They were fixated on what was wrong in their worlds. All he needed to do was to identify a problem that everyone had agreed was a problem, and the rest was history. Unfortunately for us, there was very little that we could do to remedy the unfair negative attention as well as the new rules being imposed on us. He was able to successfully get everyone to put on their "Us vs Them" blinders. This trick is highly effective. After it happened to me, I began to see it being used everywhere. The mean kids at school proactively put down other kids. They suddenly become the popular cool ones and all of their flaws and imperfections go away. Our political environments are ridiculed by such behavior. Let's face it, candidates that decide to take the "high road" typically have to fight harder to be successful. Love him or hate him, President Donald Trump is one of the best I've seen at using this tactic. Coming up with pet names for each of his opponents and accompanying his name-calling with claims of their unacceptable behavior or status. We all remember the "Crooked Hillary" and "Lying Ted" monikers. As to the How? and Why? this type of strategy works on human beings we will leave to a social psychologist or sociologist to explain. For the purpose of this book, we will just identify it as a tool that is regularly used in our society. Often times the ones using it have seen favorable results. Simply put, if you want to gain popularity and prestige in your social group, all you have to do locate a common enemy of the group and be the leading force against said enemy. More than likely they will love you for it. Even if they don't, how will they behave towards the common enemy that you have just emphasized? This last question is most relevant to our society and how we as losers interact within it. Is your behavior being manipulated for or against certain groups on the account of this phenomenon?

Looking at my example as a manager, the other manager was so successful at his tactic because he was able to draw significant lines of distinctions between the two groups. He could have very well worked along with me and the company I worked for. Assimilation was not his goal. You see, the more division he created meant the more success he was able to realize. The more success he had at presenting the enemy as an "other", the more he was able to deter everyone's interest away from him and his behavior. If we truly open our eyes, we are able to see this every day. There are white people and then black people. There are republicans and there are democrats. There are the rich and the poor. There are those that work and those who get everything free. There are those with tenure and those without tenure. There are the college-educated and the ones who didn't go to college. I could go on and on for days. Sure, we as a society are going to have our differences. These differences are essentially what makes up our many social groups. However, it is a mistake to fail to consider how these differences accompanied by the tactic just conveyed can be used against us in efforts to control our behavior. When this happens we may not even be aware that we are being manipulated. Each one of us has had on our "Us v/s Them" blinders. If our goal is to be losers that win, we must be on the lookout for such manipulative strategies. It is important to do so in order to be in full control of our own ideas and behaviors as well as to hold other people accountable for their behaviors and conditions. In whatever endeavors we choose to engage in our lives, we want to be associated with individuals who are contributing to our cause. Even though manipulating peoples' behavior is a skillset that has its place in many arenas, typically we are more interested in having people around that are valuable on the account of their contributions. In my example, a real opportunity was missed for the two companies to work together effectively on the account of one individual who was incapable of contributing to our shared success anyways. Losers who win must refrain from being duped into such disruptive frame of minds and activities. We must maintain our own critical minds at all times.

Puppets like Pinocchio

I assume that not many of us in society like the thought of ourselves as being puppets. The title of this book is called How Losers Win. My goal is not to appease your current ideals of how society works or where you fit into it. My goal is the opposite. If you are a loser who wants to win, you have to change your current mindset. You have to rip away all the junk that society and its various entities and interests have placed in your psyche and embrace the inner loser that resides in your mind, body, and soul. There is a line from Pinocchio that stands out. It was when Pinocchio said this.

"I'd rather be smart than be an actor."

This may not sound like such an extraordinary quote at first, but it has real power. I am drawing parallels between a wooden puppet character who is being controlled by strings to people in society whose mindsets are being controlled by intangible things. Yet, control is control. If we genuinely aren't acting on behalf of our pure selves in society, then we are all actors. Knowledge is power and the only way to ensure that we are not actors is to be smart about things just as Pinocchio desires. If you haven't seen the movie or read the book, I would advise you to do so. If you aren't open-minded enough to consider such a "silly" source for guidance then I would ask you what sources would you consider sufficient? Is it the education system where the teaching criteria is determined by our governing bodies? Perhaps it's your favorite cable news shows which very existence relies on major corporations' advertising dollars? Maybe it is from those in society who have unknowingly been influenced by all the manipulative stimuli present around them, or even worse someone using a specific tactic on you to alter your mindset and behavior. Like it or not, we live in a society that is a lot like the one experienced by the character Pinocchio. Our goals are the same as his, to become a real boy or girl. In order to do just that, we must remove the ideals that are in our minds that do not belong to us. Pinocchio had his strings and we have our society's ideals. Once we remove these foreign ideas, we must stay on guard to ensure that alien ideas don't make their way back into our psyche again. This is the only way that we can be mentally free in our society. Please note that everything society brings us is not the enemy of our minds. From a socioeconomic standpoint, I am referring to the ideals that are being deployed in our society that keeps us in a certain place. These ideals have many forms. They could be implanted in the behavior of our culture, the government programs, or even through our beloved celebrity's messages. Regardless of the source, we must keep watch on what we allow to sink into our thought processes. With the knowledge of what's out there and all the various intentions, with time and practice, it will become much easier to keep such infractions at bay.

MENTAL FREEDOM IS WHAT NOW?

Pinocchio's story is a very interesting one. Once he no longer had strings attached, he had to deal with something that determined how he lived his life. If he told a lie his nose would grow longer. If only we had something similar to notify us when we weren't being true to ourselves. Remember, unless we decide to live off the grid, we will never really be able to rid ourselves of the forces seeking to control our behavior as Pinocchio did. This means that we could be further manipulated at any given time. In fact, millions and millions of dollars are being spent every day for that very purpose. Our noses won't grow in length to let us know that we are in essence lying to ourselves when we behave a certain way. This means that we are constantly at war. Better stated, we are always engaging in a Revolution against the powers that wish to determine how we live our lives. As losers, breaking these mental restrictions is necessary for us to win. Without being truly free from them, we will have to contend with our own human reactions to the contrarian behavior we must embark on in order to win. It is one thing to deal with external forces pulling against us and another altogether when these forces are coming from within ourselves. Now that you know that you are engaging in a revolution, let's examine just what it is shall we.

Revolution: *A forcible overthrow of a government or social order, in favor of a new system.*

So we are referring to a revolution of our minds. Our minds control our thinking, thinking controls ideals, ideals control behaviors, behaviors dictate habits, habits determine socioeconomic outcomes. If our goal is to win in the socioeconomic game as losers, then, when considering this progression, it is imperative that we first have complete control of our minds. We must become free like Pinocchio so that we can control our own destinies. Make no mistake about it, it is entirely possible to be a loser and to take the loser route all while your actions are being manipulated by society and others. Many losers are living this way every day. Many of you may be doing so as well. Being mentally free means you must through your own individual revolution reject the social order currently present and develop your new system. This means that every ideal that came from your past will need to be carefully examined to determine if it is a genuine ideal of your own. It also means that you will need to begin monitoring the external stimuli that you engage with moving forward. We are only human beings, meaning we have a limited amount of capabilities. Once again, I will leave the specifics to how brainwashing and human influence work to the professionals, but generally speaking if we consume enough stimuli of a particular message it's only a matter of time before we will be affected by it. So yes, it is important to pay attention to what we let into our minds. Even when information makes its way to our minds we must make it a point to carefully examine it. We must also be mindful of the people we associate with. Some of the people in our lives will undoubtedly send us in the wrong direction in regards to our revolution. We need to either limit or cut out those people from our lives. This could be our beloved friends or family members many of which will mean a great deal to us. We must carefully examine just how much winning means to us. Maybe the answer is to sit down and have a long conversation with these individuals where you ask them to respect your ambitions and refrain from violating the boundaries you set in your interactions. Regardless of how this is done, in order to truly revolutionize your mind and take full control of your thinking you will need to have a working knowledge and control of how stimulus enters your psyche as well as how you should be interacting with it.

Social Suicide

The world around us, what we refer to as our society, will not like the changes your mental revolution will require. Yet, in order to become mentally free, a revolution is required. Let me tell you here and now that it will more likely than not isolate you from society. From society, its people, and its institutions' vantage point, not only are you deciding to abandon your ambitions to become a winner, you are rejecting its messages and behaviors too! Many people may see you and your presence to be social suicide for their own sake. Don't be surprised if no one is showing up to the gatherings you put together or if you aren't getting many likes on social media. Remember, if this is the case take it as a sign that you are on the right track. You will never achieve a different outcome from others by repeating their activities. It just so happens that society is very sensitive that way. It's what makes society work. It needs its norms and rules and thus often strong reactions to those rules being broken or abandoned in order to remain relevant. You should try to understand this and never take it personally. You are simply on a different path. A path that most in society don't understand or even believe in. Many people out there in society, who aren't losers, will hold true the notion that the American Dream is to be had by the type of behavior that is required for one to be a societal winner. Don't be surprised at your inability to convince them otherwise. I am not dogmatic enough to advocate that what is in this book is right and that their beliefs are wrong. My claim is that the ideas in this book are better for losers who want to win. There are plenty of sources out there written on behalf of winners who are seeking to win. This is not one of those sources. This book is for losers like myself. I have had to come to terms with the fact that I am not in harmony with the majority of people in society. This fact has its consequences. I knew that I was not going to win social butterfly awards while I embarked on my ambitious goals to win as a loser. The best thing to do when dealing with these certain circumstances is to embrace them. Develop a sense of elitism in your own mind if you must. You more than likely will not have an extensive support system in your endeavors. Therefore it is entirely up to you to take care of your state of being. Coming to the realization that you are and will be ok in your efforts is a major part of this. As losers, we have to be the players, coach, crowd, and our own cheerleaders if we are going to win. Many others in society will undoubtedly take on the appearance of our opponents. Your challenge is to prepare yourself, stay on course, and never take it personally.

New Found Power

Obtaining mental freedom isn't all bad, I promise. Yes, you will probably lose plenty of social stock if you choose to actively reject societies' ideas and behaviors. However, I would like to contend that you will gain a newfound power in doing so. The line from the original movie Child's Play comes to mind when the villain used a voodoo chant to place his soul in the body of a Chucky Doll. With his arm raised up to the sky, he proclaimed "GIVE ME THE POWER I BEG OF YOU!" In truth the newfound power that you will harness by removing the constant influence and manipulations of society on your actions and ideas is enormous. You will be able to see with your own minds' eye that which is unseen by others. As a loser who is seeking to win, you will not be choosing a path that has already been cleared by the masses. You will be blazing your own trail. Having a clear and concise perception and a keen knowledge of not only what is currently happening but also the ability to pick up on what is really going on behind the scenes will be vital to your efforts to win.

Power of Individuals

In the previous chapter, I listed several individuals who were losers and ended up not only winning, but that won big. The power of individuals to make changes in the world we live in is great once they are no longer connected to the matrix so-to-speak. Society can't help but notice when a member goes against the grain. It usually reacts by rejecting the person portraying such actions. Society also can't help but pay attention to individuals who have gone against the grain and realized major accomplishments. This means that losers who think and act for themselves are in a unique position to make a huge impact. In many historical texts, you can find stories of individuals who were first rejected by everyone as they began to deviate from the rest of society. Later we find that these same individuals went on to have very large amounts of people in the same society following them or their cause. Even though society and its groups are prone to reject any actors that fail to act according to the acceptable syntax code, it usually grabs hold of its programming bugs that prove themselves to be valuable. They typically take hold of society and spread as viruses do. This enables losers who stick to their ambitions and goals to have tremendous potential upside to their actions. With this upside, they, even as individuals, can make major changes and have a real long-lasting impact on the world.

If you are fortunate enough to have a group of losers and likeminded individuals who, along with you are set on innovating society, you will have increased your potential impact exponentially. As humans, it's in our nature to learn from the behavior of others. We tune in to other peoples' outcomes when considering our own actions. Years ago, seeing other human beings suddenly die after eating a certain wild berry would no doubt cause the rest of the group to reconsider eating that particular wild berry. What if it was only one individual that ate the berry and died? It is then not clear as to what caused the sudden death. It could have been something he did yesterday, or it could just be an underlying medical issue he had for a while that caused him to die just now. In this oversimplified example, it is easy to see the power that human beings harness when behaving in concert. It is essentially the same way that society works. A large number of people embark on behaviors so that the individual has the benefit of engaging less when making the decision of whether to do the action. This is how social change can spread like wildfire once a number of people have caught on to an idea. Furthermore, the more diverse the group, the greater the impact on society. The society we live in is made up of thousands of groups that we differentiate ourselves from. Eliminating these differences as much as possible is one way of maximizing the impact of your efforts.

Let's be real. As losers who have not yet won, you will face an uphill battle in your efforts to be successful and gain favor in society. This will be the case no matter how good your idea is, how right you are, or how good you are at what you do. These things just don't matter when it comes to the social behavioral order of a society. Then things will only get worse for you when you decide to form your own revolution in your mind and unplug yourself from the matrix and all its influences. Generally speaking, you will be the last person that people will flock to offering help or looking to fall in line with your ambitions. However, this does not necessarily mean that you will be at a disadvantage. In the bestselling author Malcolm Gladwell's book called David and Goliath, he challenged the notion that our perceived underdogs are actually underdogs at all. He suggests that in many cases, the unfortunate situations that they often find themselves in are essentially the very reason that they are able to find success. According to Gladwell, these same individuals, if immersed in a more favorable circumstance probably wouldn't have gone on to do the amazing things that they ended up doing. I would like to echo this concept here. As losers, each and every one of you is in a unique position to do amazing things. The contrary would be to strive to be a winner where you will be joined by millions of millions of people who will be your competition. I realize that competition is a good thing and those who operate in that arena and end up on top often provide many needed contributions that propel our society forward. However, it still remains true that standing indifference with convention often presents unique opportunities. It can also be said that it creates a unique opportunity to make changes as you will most definitely not blend in with the crowd. The often controversial rapper Tupac Shakur seemed to understand this when he came out with his work titled "All Eyes on Me". With his, say what is on his mind, style that unapologetically challenged the establishment, he was not one that would be confused with someone attempting to blend in. On the account of his behavior and willingness to go against the grain, the world paid more attention to his work. To this day he is considered by many to be one of the greatest rappers ever despite his death at the young age of 25. This is not to say that anyone can make some noise going against the grain and no matter what they are pursuing it will be successful. In fact, this couldn't be further from the truth. A lot must go into whatever you are working on in life. The age-old saying that nothing worth having comes easy rings true. However, if you put forth the work and effort and stick to your own guns then what may seem to be a disadvantage can very well be the exact opposite. There is great power in being a loser who puts in the work and remains unplugged from the matrix. I am certain that each one of you is anxious to do just that. However, we still have some unfinished business to attend to. We've already identified you as a proud loser of our society. Good for you! We've just finished talking about how you too can become a real boy or girl just as Pinocchio did by unplugging and keeping yourself unplugged from societies' matrix. What about this hard work though? How do you even know what you should be doing? Should you just pick at random? Uh, the answer is absolutely not! That would be a recipe for disaster! All you losers who want to win, I'll see you in the next chapter where we discuss how to identify what YOU should be working on in your efforts to win.

CHAPTER 3:

Me, Myself, & I

"Men can starve from a lack of self-realization as much as they can from a lack of bread."

-Richard Wright

Mirror, Mirror, on the Wall

In the laundry list of activities that I have engaged with over the years, one of them was writing poetry. I wrote a poem years ago that's a perfect fit for the beginning of this chapter.

Untitled

What happens when I no longer feel myself and all memories of me have vanished?

Do I become anew or simply another who?

Wishing that me is who I am but without a point of reference to identify I, I can only wonder

If or not me truly exist

In a world where different versions of yourself are handed out at every single turn

It's too easy to become confused

All of the clutter blocking your way

As all the noise impairs your hearing

Simplified to the least common denominator

We are all made up of us

The very same ingredients are present

In an ever recycling events of regeneration

Yet still, I feel

As though, I don't know

If I'm actually me, or another version

I'll call him he or she

They look just like us in every shape form or fashion

Can even mimic our passions

To pull a fools eye over our own eyes

So that we come to a full stop with our whys?

One can never really know for sure

As nothing stays the same except change

So change I shall or shall I not?

Looking for an ever so present sign to show me, me

Sometimes forgetting to ask why, I present my question mark today

Does it even matter?

I wonder as all the chatter tempts me to listen

It must! I scream at the top of my lungs!

If it doesn't matter then we are all one

Which makes us worthless

And significantly insignificant

Not a fate that I want for I

This is why, each and every I must always be searching for me

Through the dense forest and the treacherous sea

Drop kicking him, punching out her, and overcoming he

All for the sake of our I, we must all find and keep our me!

This poem raises a very important question. With all of the external influences of the world we live in, how do we know who we actually are? I mean do we really like a certain pair of sneakers or is it because Lebron James cosigns for them and many others in society value them? If that same shoe was not associated with Lebron and it was under a brand that we had never heard of what would we have said about that shoe then? Some may think we choose brands that we know on account of the quality. Using the same shoe example, do we even know if the brand Lebron endorses is of a higher quality than the brand we haven't heard of? Chances are we have not done enough research to make that claim. Therefore, how are we making the decision to choose our sneakers or our cars, our clothing, our food, our hair and makeup products, our soft drinks, our toothpaste and soap, our washing detergent,... I could go on and on. This doesn't just end with our consumer purchases. How are we really making dating decisions? How do we really decide who becomes our friends or our enemies? Are our choices of vacation really our own? If we are not aware of the powers manipulating us in the processes we use to make our shoe purchases, then chances are we use the same process when making many other decisions in our lives. So the question as asked in the poem above is not just who am I, but also how do I know that I am actually me?

To Each Their Own Way

There is no one way of assessing who you are. To be clear, what I mean by who you are in this context comes down to what you should embark on in your efforts to win socioeconomically. Each one of you losers out there will have to find that out for yourself. What I will be doing in this chapter is providing you with some (absolutely not all) tools to help you in your efforts to find your thing(s). I began my journey of self-discovery years ago yet only recently have I been able to fully understand and apply my findings to my life. The problem was that I did not yet think of myself as a loser and had not yet unplugged myself from society's matrix. I wasn't starting from scratch so everything that I learned about myself, I applied to where it fitted in with my efforts to become a winner or where it fitted in with my compromised ideals. That is the reason this chapter on finding your true self comes only after you have read and understood the previous 2 chapters. In order to be a loser who wins, you must be winning at your uninhibited game and on your uninhibited terms. Otherwise, you will realize that you end up working towards a goal that you aren't motivated to embark on. Even worse, if you aren't working towards what you genuinely want to do, you may end up arriving at a version of success that you do not desire to have. It took me a very long while to accept my loser status and to shed all the baggage that society was instilling in my mind, but once I did, I was able to clearly see not just what I should do, but how I should do it. And guess what? It became easier than anything else I had previously attempted to do. I was literally a natural at doing the thing I was built to do. Who knew! This is what I want for all of you. This is the last chapter of the first section of this book which consists of altering your internal framework. Only after you have changed the way you are on the inside can you change the way you behave with honesty and integrity. We are now at the last step of this process. Let's do the work of getting you started on finding out just who you really are!

Your Values

Do you know what it is that you value? This may seem like a silly question, but let's not forget how society has a way of providing answers to these very personal questions for us. If we aren't careful we can adopt the values of a person, group, or organization and pass it along as our own without realizing it. So again I ask, do you know what you value?

Value: *a person's principles or standards of behavior; one's judgment of what is important in life.*

The second part of the definition really strikes me. One's own judgment of what is important in their life. Now when we throw in the first part of the definition it all comes together. Essentially what I am asking you when inquiring about your values is what have you identified as important to you in your life in regards to your behavior and who or what you are associated with? Applying it to socioeconomics, someone may have an opportunity to make a good living for themselves doing work that they thoroughly enjoy. However, if the work requires them to behave in a way that contradicts what is important in their life they will probably pass on the opportunity. There is no right or wrong answer here. Don't feel as though you are obligated to have values at all when it comes to your work. It is just important to start here in order to identify any barriers or necessities that you may have in regards to the values you hold before moving forward. If you are not sure of what values you hold dear, I suggest that you go online and search for core value assessments. You can find many online that are absolutely free. In the meantime below I have provided a list of core values for you. Look over this list and jot down the top 3-5 values or so that are essential to the way that you live your life. You will encounter core values that you like or simply wish to avoid. I recommend that you don't include those in your list. This exercise is to identify a shortlist of your core values so only add a value to your list if you have very strong feelings about it. For example, you may enjoy occasionally interacting with the people in your community and be tempted to add community as one of your core values. However, unless working in or on behalf of your community is a part of who you are I would leave it off the list.

CORE VALUES

Authenticity	Achievement	Adventure	Authority
Autonomy	Balance	Beauty	Boldness
Compassion	Challenge	Citizenship	Community
Competency	Contribution	Creativity	Curiosity
Determination	Fairness	Faith	Fame
Friendships	Fun	Growth	Happiness

Honesty	Humor	Influence	Inner Harmony
Justice	Kindness	Knowledge	Leadership
Learning	Love	Loyalty	Meaningful Work
Openness	Optimism	Peace	Pleasure
Poise	Popularity	Recognition	Religion
Reputation	Respect	Responsibility	Security
Self-Respect	Service	Spirituality	Stability
Success	Status	Trustworthiness	Wealth & Wisdom

This is by no means an exhaustive list of values. You should also write down any core values you know that you have or any that you may find in your internet search should you choose to do so. Once you have these values written down, they will serve as an authentic source of information defining who you are as a person. You should also revisit the list from time to time as your values may change over time as you experience more things in your life.

Your Passion(s)

Now that you have identified your core values, do you know what you are passionate about? Where Values determine how you desire to behave according to your strongly held beliefs, Passions determine what you feel driven to do. You may have an emotional response when you see certain things going on in the world and feel that you need to do something about it. This is not to say that passions have to be targeted towards social causes. Someone could be just as passionate about their work, working out, or playing a musical instrument for example. On the other hand, it is perfectly ok if you find that you don't possess any passions at this time in your life. Do not make up one or adopt a passion you think you should have. The passion or passions that you identify with must be ones that you resonate with.

Just like you did with your values, jot down your passion(s) and keep it in a place where you can easily access it at all times. If you have authentically identified both your values and your passions then you have tangible evidence of who you truly are as a person. This evidence will come in handy if you ever begin to lose your way or begin to get swayed by society and its many influences.

Your Skills

I once heard that if you do something for 10,000 plus hours, you will be considered an expert at said thing. I do not know if this is true, but when considering skills it does bring up an important concept. The concept that the more one does something the better that they become at it. In other words, the more work you put into something the better you will be at it. I am sure there is some validity to this concept but there is still a lot of gray areas when considering the extremely subjective topic of skill.

For the sake of this book, we will not go too deep into whether or not you actually have a skill at something. I mean there are just too many variables. If you are the sole judge, you can be absolutely biased for or against your work. If we rely on what others think, social factors can play too large a role in the determination of your skillset. A bad writer may have supportive friends and family members who decide to appease him by telling him his work is brilliant. At the same time, a great writer may have friends and family who are hating on her and tell her that her work sucks. Things could get even more complicated if we began to analyze the perception of good versus bad writing within each group of friends and family members.

For the sake of this book, we will not overthink the concept of skillset. However, we do want to be as authentic as possible. This will serve better in your efforts to you win. If you identify a skill that is actually not one, chances are that your efforts will hit a brick wall. To remedy this what I want you to do is to consider how much time you have put into a skill, your perception of the skill, as well as other peoples' perception of it. Having done so, just as you did with your values and passions, jot down your list of skills so that you can easily assess them at any time in the future.

Your Interest

There is this phenomenon referred to as being in a state of Flow. Before I heard of this concept I heard it referred to as being "in the zone". It is essentially when someone is so engaged in an activity that they temporarily lose their state of being. They lose track of time and are said to be performing at their most optimum level. Think of the athlete who "blacks out" and just can't be stopped. They are so immersed in what they are doing that they have difficulty explaining what they did after they did it. This is an extreme example of Flow, but I wanted to start there because I wanted to make a point about your interest. I want you to jot down your interests just as we have done with your values, passions, and skills. However, I do not want you to write down every single thing that you are interested in. For many of us that would be such a long list that there would be no value therein identifying who we are and what we like. What I want you to do is to consider the things that you embark on that you get lost in. The things that cause you to forget to eat when you are engaged. The things that you consistently find yourself wanting to do when you are finally done with tasks that you struggle to get through. Your interests must resonate with you at a level that you often find yourself in a state of flow or constantly in the zone when you are doing them. You may have one, ten, or zero things that you engage with this level of interest and that is perfectly fine. The main thing is to be as authentic as possible. Do not feel pressure to come up with something. You will only be doing yourself a disservice by presenting an unauthentic representation. As with the other measures, write down your interests and put in a place where it is always accessible. Your interest is another one that you will want to revisit occasionally as it may change with time as you experience more things in your life.

Your VIPS

Congratulations! You have just completed your VIPS! Your VIPS (Very Important Perception of Self). It consists of your Values-Interests-Passions-Skills. These four parameters combined provide you with the story of the unique person that you are. No two VIPS will be the same. Your VIPS will always serve to help you make authentic decisions in your life. If you haven't already, combine all four elements on a single document. It could be a handwritten sheet of paper or an electronic document on the cloud. The key is to always have it where you can assess it. Memorize it if you are capable of doing so. The next time you are faced with a major decision consult with your VIPS. If done correctly, it will never steer you wrong. I started doing this a while ago and it didn't take long for me to realize how I was making decisions in my life that were unauthentic to who I actually was. Once you begin to use your personalized VIPS, I am certain that it will change your life as it did mine.

Myers Briggs Personality Type

If you have already heard of and know your Myers Briggs Personality Type you can go on to the next section. If you have not heard of Myers Briggs then I present to you a tool that can help you discover more about yourself. This tool helped me realize that I was not alone in the way that I thought, felt, and behaved. The Myers Briggs system is essentially an instrument that looks at 4 select human preferences and categorizes them into 16 different types. Complete the following basic assessment I have created for you to identify your Myers Briggs Personality type. With each answer, copy the corresponding letter in the parenthesis behind the answer. You will only have one letter per question. After you have completed your assessment, you will have your 4-letter Myers Briggs type. For example, if you answered Introverted for question number 1 you will write down the letter "I". If your answer to question number 2 is Ideas, then you will add the letter "N" to your results to give you "IN". If "Your logic" was your answer to question number 3 and "weeks early" was your answer to question number 4, you will add the letters "T" and "J" to your results giving you the Myers Briggs Personality Type "INTJ". This assessment is a measure of your preferences so record the response that fits you more often than the other choice.

Myers Briggs Quick Assessment

1. Are you more...?

Introverted(I) or   Extroverted(E)

2. Are you more concerned with...?

Ideas(N)   or   What you see, hear, touch, taste, & feel(S)

3. Do you mostly make decisions with...?

Logic(T)   or   Your values & beliefs(F)

4. Do you more often finish projects...?

Weeks early(J) or   At the last minute(P)

You have just found out your Myers Briggs Personality Type. Again, this is a very basic test. If you had difficulty completing this test and aren't too confident of your results, then feel free to find other sources available out there for a more precise measure. There are many free assessments all over the internet. Below is a brief description of each personality type and the type of work/careers that fit best. These short descriptions can be found at pstypes.blogspot.com.

ENTJ – THE FIELD MARSHALL

People with this personality type are generally strong, expansive, domineering, decisive, clear-cut and logical. They are very pragmatic and extraordinary strategic thinkers who have both the vision and the ability to make their vision come true. ENTJs are natural leaders, goal-oriented, innovative, determined, powerful, they like to make things happen and don't have much patience with incompetence, inefficiency, hurt feelings or any other things they believe might slow them down. They are good at directing teams and can make wonderful leaders, although at times they can be perceived by others as somewhat insensitive, argumentative and domineering. Some preferred careers are: CEO/ Executive, Lawyer/Judge, Business Consultant, Sales Manager, Venture Capitalist, Politician, and Administrator.

INTP – THE ARCHITECT

This personality type is known for being intellectual, abstract, logical, reserved, detached, random and skeptical. Such people are usually unconventional and highly theoretical, they like playing with ideas and coming up with ingenious thought systems and explanations for the events they observe, although they aren't too likely to share their discoveries, as they're quite socially withdrawn and secretive. INTPs are also objective spontaneous, adaptable and highly independent; they often question authority, openly disregard social conventions and irrational customs and prefer to think for themselves, which can lead to an original, avant-garde vision of things, but also to being perceived as arrogant, cold and eccentric. Some preferred careers are: Computer Programmer, Financial Analyst, Chemist/Biologist/Physicist, College Professor, Economist/Mathematician, Researcher, and Lawyer/Judge.

ENFJ – THE TEACHER

Individuals with this personality type are usually compassionate, understanding, insightful, open-minded, generous and altruistic, but also organized and driven, on a professional level. They are both kind and firm, are amazing public speakers and enjoy being among people, helping, understanding and guiding them through their troubles. ENFJs make exceptional friends, as they are gregarious, generous, cultivated and usually have a penetrating perception of the emotional needs of others, which they consequently feel the urge to meet. Although empathetic and affectionate, they can at times become quite demanding, controlling and excessively image-conscious. Some top careers are: Advertising Executive, Public Relations, Corporate Coach/Trainer, Human Resources/Recruiter, Writer/Journalist, Restaurant Manager, and Translator.

ENFP – THE CHAMPION

This personality type is known for being spontaneous, optimistic, creative, expansive, playful and very charismatic. They are curious people, with a great need for variety, change, adventure, and emotional engagement. Two of their best qualities are their wide imagination and their versatility – this type is a quick abstract learner, excels at brainstorming and loves having causes to believe in and work for. Naturally, ENFPs are sociable humanists who love helping and understand other people. They are warm, very friendly and generous with their time and energy, but they do have a tendency to spread themselves too thin and find it difficult to keep all their promises they make or complete all the projects they take on. Some preferred careers are: Journalist, Advertising Creative Director, Consultant, Restauranteur, Event Planner, Character Actor, and Spokesperson.

ISTJ – THE INSPECTOR

This personality type is stable, precautious, traditional, detail-oriented, practical and orderly. They are very conscientious people that can be relied upon to do a thorough job, as they take their duties very seriously and prefer things to be structured and logically ordered. Pillars of their society, ISTJs excel at working with detail (they do not mind routine as much as other types), they are precise, meticulous and very down-to-earth. They respect traditions, the longstanding values of their society, the precious lessons of history and also the hierarchical structure of people and things. Although honest and hard-working, they may be perceived by others as a bit old-fashioned, tedious and frugal. Some preferred careers are: Veterinarian, Accountant/Auditor, Manager/Administrator, Chief Financial officer, Web Development Engineer, Government Employee, and Physician.

ISTP – THE CRAFTER

People with this personality type are typically independent, individualistic, practical, handy, audacious and very realistic. They are adaptable and casual, trust their own experience and are very skillful at coordinating their minds with their bodies, which makes them wonderful at handling different tools or working with equipment and machinery. Their freedom and autonomy are highly important to them so they prefer working independently and keeping demands on their person to a minimum. ISTPs are also very rational, straight forward people who usually keep to themselves and dislike social pressure, things that may actually cause them difficulties in their relationships, occasionally being perceived as inconsiderate, selfish and unreliable. Some top careers are: Civil Engineer, Pilot, Computer Specialist, Data Communications Analyst, Emergency Room Physician, Intelligence Agent, and Geologist.

ISFJ – THE PROTECTOR

People who have this personality type are generally kind, empathetic, traditional, shy, caring, practical and very loyal. They love helping and assisting others around them and often assume a nurturing role in their family and society, as they make wonderful caregivers and mother-figures. Often self-effacing and unpretentious, they, in fact, have very strong moral convictions and a deep-seated sense of their social and human duty and purpose. ISFJs are very affectionate, committed and dedicated to their loved ones and they are often willing to sacrifice their own wishes and needs in order to meet those of others, which may eventually end up causing them a fair amount of emotional suffering and frustration, in the long run. Some top careers are: Physician/Dentist, Dietitian/Nutritionist, Elementary School Teacher, Nurse, Librarian, Franchise Owner, and Customer Service representative.

ESFP – THE PERFORMER

This personality type is known for being active, outgoing, happy-go-lucky, talkative, fun-loving, trustful and friendly. They very much appreciate and enjoy the tangible reality around them – they like to be physically active, to interact with other people and to have a lot of fun (music, art, shopping, partying, sports, are only some of their many interests). ESFPs are also loyal, affectionate and spirited people, they know how to tune into other people's emotional states and match their expectations and therefore they easily become very popular wherever they go. Born entertainers, they relish having an audience and being in the spotlight, but they can also become overly dramatic, demonstrative, frivolous and whimsical, especially when they are not getting the attention they desire. Some top careers are: Child Counselor/Child Care, Primary Care Physician, Film Producer/Actor, Sales Representative, Travel Agent, Receptionist/Secretary, and Waiter/Waitress.

INTJ – THE MASTERMIND

This personality type is withdrawn, intellectual, reflective, unconventional, abstract, insightful and methodical. These people are typically hard to read and tend to come across as dispassionate, unemotional, quirky, yet very self-controlled. Their most treasured pursuit is the one for knowledge, for the fundamental truth behind appearances and INTJs have a natural flair for seeking, discerning and understanding the very essence of things. While on the outside, they often appear to be logical, cautious, rational and skeptical individuals, their inner life of the mind is rich beyond belief with symbols, meaning and innovative visions of the future. Although often brilliant and ahead of their time, they are sometimes perceived by their peers as being rather strange, arrogant and distant. Some top careers are: Investment Banker, Personal Finance Advisor, Software Developer, Economist, Executive, Engineer/Architect, and Scientist.

ESFJ – THE PROVIDER

People with this personality type are kind, polite, helpful, altruistic, affectionate, traditional and friendly. They need to feel that they're a useful and appreciated part of their community; therefore they will embrace and champion the social conventions and traditions that exist in their society. Orderly, neat and well-behaved, they are always careful to appropriately fulfill their social role, as dictated by the nature of the relationships involved. ESFJs are often pleasant, gracious, sympathetic people, who love to help others in practical and tangible ways, making sure everyone is fitting in and relationships are peaceful and harmonious within their family or group. Their acute need for praise and gratitude, however, may occasionally cause others to see them as clingy, manipulative and pushy. Some top careers are: Sales Representative, Nurse/Healthcare Worker, Office Manager, PR Account Executive, Loan Officer, Flight attendant, and Athletic Coach.

ESTP – THE PROMOTER

This personality type is known for being outgoing, self-confident, entertaining, rational, pragmatic, and matter-of-fact. They like having an active lifestyle, countless friends and being up-to-date with everything that's going on in their world, as they want to always keep up with the latest trends. Fun, adventurous and charismatic, they are also highly competitive and enterprising people with well-developed tactic skills, which they often employ to gain an advantage in immediate situations. ESTPs prefer to live in the moment and rarely make long-term plans – they're spontaneous, action-oriented and quite hedonistic, with a flair for spotting opportunities and making the most out of every situation. This approach, however, can make some people regard them as irresponsible, superficial and inconsiderate. Some top careers are: Detective/Police Officer, Banker/Auditor/Stock Broker, Entertainment Agent/Promoter, Sports Coach/Pro Athlete, General Contractor, Entrepreneur, and Marking Professional.

INFP – THE HEALER

People who have this personality type are generally reserved, tolerant, idealistic, sympathetic, insightful, romantic, natural and unplanned. They are avidly searching for the inner beauty of nature and people, the harmonious balance of life and the true value of everything around them. Intensely imaginative, intuitive and open-minded, they easily perceive the human potential that's hidden behind appearances and become inspired by it. INFPs are empathetic listeners, genuinely interested in what other people have to say, but at the same time, their need for privacy and introspection can make them retreat from social contact in order to process their feelings undisturbed. This emotional sensitivity can sometimes make them appear as unsociable, moody and illogical. Some top careers are: Graphic Designer/Artist, Psychologist/Therapist, Writer/Editor/Reporter, Minister/Priest/Missionary, Human Resources/Trainer, Curator, and Actor/Musician/Composer.

ESTJ – THE SUPERVISOR

Individuals with this personality type are realistic, practical, organized, hard-working, conventional, responsible, outgoing and assertive. They are very rational people who trust and follow clear logical principles and tend to approach every situation in an objective and impartial manner. Highly realistic and driven, their energy is often invested in pursuits that have a practical application and a tangible result. Their stable, industrious personality is based on a deep-seated sense of duty towards the social system they are a part of and the established rules attached to it. Although, earnest, loyal and respectful to their society, ESTJs are also strong, decisive people, who can lead and organize others confidently. As a result, they can sometimes be perceived as quite rigid, tactless and domineering by those around them. Some top careers are: Insurance Agent, Pharmacist, Lawyer/Judge, School Administrator, Project Manager, Police/Military Officer, or Bank Manager.

INFJ – THE COUNSELLOR

This personality type is generally very private, empathetic, wise, thoughtful, profound, romantic and complex. They have rich inner worlds, fostered by their wide imagination, which reflect their love for abstract symbols and spiritual meaning. Their insightful understanding of human nature makes them talented at exploring and capturing the subtle emotional truths of the human experience (often through beautiful artistic creations). INFJs are sympathetic, humanitarian individuals, who strive for harmony, cooperation and unity among people, yet their reserved, introspective nature eventually urges them to seek privacy in order to sort out their feeling and ideas. Although wise and insightful, their emotional complexity can sometimes make them appear as overly sensitive, moody and strange. Some top careers are: Therapist/Psychologist, Social Worker, Human Resources, Organizational Consultant, Mediator, Customer Relations Manager, and Clergy/Minister.

ISFP – THE COMPOSER

People with this personality type are known for being gentle, compassionate, uncomplicated, spontaneous, natural, peaceful and modest. They highly value their personal freedom and need plenty of private time and space, in which to follow their calling, very often represented by nature and artistic activities. Kind, generous and sensitive, ISFPs often have developed emotional intelligence and are gifted at correctly reading the body language and unexpressed feelings of those around them. Their warm and empathetic nature, as well as their need for harmony and serenity, will drive them to help those in need or in suffering, usually in concrete and tangible ways. Despite their childlike joy and playfulness, they can be regarded by some as hesitant, soft and naive. Some top careers are: Fashion Designers, Physical Therapist, Landscape Architect, Storekeeper/Clerk, Chef, Beautician, and Archaeologist.

ENTP – THE INVENTOR

People with this personality type are usually optimistic, outgoing, inventive, logical, playful, spontaneous and humorous. They are quick-minded, rational and flexible and they find it easy to improvise and come up with a multitude of ideas and solutions, which can make them ingenious problem solvers and even pioneers in their fields of interest. Their adventurousness and openness to new experiences, combined with their sociable, fun-loving nature often make them widely popular and well-liked by many of their peers. But despite their cheerfulness and carefree attitude, ENTPs often harbor a sharp, strategic mind and they are perfectly capable of detaching from their feelings in order to pragmatically reach their objectives. This very aspect can make some people regard them as unpredictable, insensitive and egotistical. Some top careers are: Entrepreneur, Venture Capitalist, Advertising/Marking Director, Politician/Political Consultant, Strategic Planner, Market Researcher, and Management Consultant.

Now That You Know You

Alright, my fellow losers. Equipped with your very own VIPS and your Myers Briggs Personality Type, you are well on your way to be the true authentic author of your own life. The sky is the limit as to what you can achieve for yourself. By declaring yourself a loser, rejecting society's manipulative forces, and doing the work to find out just what you are truly made of, there is nothing in the way of you being absolutely socially free! Congratulations are definitely in order! However, I did promise that by the end of this book, you would know how to be a loser that wins. Although gaining social freedom is the most significant part, which is why I have spent so much relative time on it, we have reached the part of this book where you will learn the other part of the equation. Starting in the next section we will begin the discussion on how a loser like you can win by becoming financially free.

CHAPTER 4:

Mind Your Own Beeswax

"Today as always, men fall into two groups: slaves and free men. Whoever does not have two-thirds of his day for himself, is a slave, whatever he may be: a statesman, a businessman, an official, or a scholar."

-Friedrich Nietzsche

Whips & Chains

Have a look at the definition of the word slave.

SLAVE – noun

> 1. : a person held in servitude as the chattel of another
> 2. : one that is completely subservient to a dominating influence

This definition really strikes me because it does not mention the word contract, chains, bondage, or any other physical instrument that comes to my mind when I think of slavery. In fact, the second part of the definition simply states a condition of being. That condition being completely subservient. The word subservient defined as an adjective is as follows.

SUBSERVIENT – prepared to obey others unquestioningly.

Unquestioningly is the keyword here. The definition continues on to mention a dominating influence as the entity the subservient behavior adheres to. Again, this definition falls extremely short of what I had been considering to have been slavery. Yet it makes sense. All of the other more identifiable instruments of intimidation, in practice, were only used to enforce slavery. If they were not necessary, they wouldn't exist. Thus, they are simply instruments used to enforce the mindset of slavery on to the slave. Therefore, slavery is essentially a mindset. You may be wondering why I am bringing this up. Slavery in the United States has been outlawed, right? But I have a question for you...How do you outlaw an idea? How can you make a mindset illegal? You cannot! This means that slavery in many forms could be alive and well right here in today's time. Let's look at the definition of a slave one more time.

SLAVE – noun

      1. : a person held in servitude as the chattel of another
      2. : one that is completely subservient to a dominating influence

All that is necessary for you or me to be a slave is to be completely subservient (which means to obey unquestionably) to a dominating influence. This dominating influence would actually be better served in its efforts to have us as slaves if it did not use in its tactics those horrible ideas we have in our minds as to what slavery is. The gig would no doubt be over if we got even a slimmer of a hint that some entity was attempting to enslave us, right? This is why a clever plot would be necessary to disguise the true intentions of anyone looking to enslave another this day in time. I think such a clever plot is present in the capitalistic system in the United States' economy. Let me just say again, I am not one for conspiracy theories. I am not claiming that there is an evil mastermind or evil group present somewhere in the shadows that has the sole purpose to enslave us all as a part of some evil sick plot. What I am simply stating is that the way our economic system is set up and has been running for over a century has all the pieces to support the existence of slavery according to the definition. Let me go back in history a bit, to the time of slavery, in order to provide a foundational premise for my claim. Have you ever heard of Willie Lynch?

Willie Lynch's Letter

During the time of slavery in the United States, a foreigner by the name of Willie Lynch went on a tour giving a speech. He was known as a prominent slave owner where he was from and had much success in breaking slaves. Breaking refers to the turning wild or troublesome slaves into money producing pieces of property. Well, this speech was eventually written up into a letter and distributed throughout the country. Here is an insert from Willie Lynch's letter that is extremely interesting and I think relevant to this day in our capitalistic system.

In making a slave...

"...We will use the same basic principle that we use in breaking a horse, combined with some more sustaining factors. What we do with horses is that we break them from one form of life to another that is we reduce them from their natural state in nature. Whereas nature provides them with the natural capacity to take care of their offspring, we break that natural string of independence from them and thereby create a dependency status, so that we may be able to get from them useful production for our business and pleasure."

Do you know of any people who are so dependent on working for a company that they do not believe that they have the natural capacity to take care of themselves and their offspring without their jobs? It is one thing to know that you are capable of taking care of yourself and your family and making a choice to work for a business, but another thing altogether to believe that you do not have such capacity. Willie Lynch stated as fact that nature provides us all with the natural capacity to take care of ourselves and those we care about. This is the case not only when considering using land to grow food or wood from trees to build shelter, but also included in the capacity to engage in enterprise and social arrangements. Either way, we all have the capacity in nature to provide for ourselves. Yet, many of us to this day do not consider that to be the case. We instead feel that we have to work for another entity in order to survive. The owners of the firms in society that provides us with the jobs are the dominating influences that we unquestionably obey.

Have any of you ever wondered why it is that we as the people applying for a jobs at an interviews are the ones in the hot seat? We think, how we can best impress the interviewer? We make sure that we learn as much as we can about the company just in case we are asked certain questions. We get nervous and feel as though we have failed if we don't elude the right amounts of confidence and humility or if we stumble on our words. Meanwhile, the interviewer oftentimes looks at us as we are inferior. We have to prove ourselves worthy. We don't question this process at all do we? All in society just fall in line with it. Sure, they may hold a few positions and may have more applicants than they can handle which would cause for a swift elimination process. Yet, it still does not account for the extremely skewed hierarchical relationship. The truth of the matter is that the company is seeking to hire someone to either make them money or to protect their assets. The cost of which to them in salary will not exceed the worth of the person they eventually hire. In other words, as a potential hire, we who are applying for the job should not be so nervous. If anything, the employer should be a little on edge. The interviewer should feel the pressure of attempting to persuade you and me into making his firm money, right? Well, this is more often not the case and we, as a society fail to question it. We simply fall in line. The reason why we do it? Oh, because in our capitalistic society, many of us have come to believe that we need a job working for another person's company in order to survive. I mentioned tricky being necessary this day in time for slavery to exist remember? We know what slavery looks like and will react accordingly if faced with the prospects today. Well, a clever thing about working for a company in today's' society is that we usually don't even consider the fact that we are actually working for another person or a group of people. How is that for pulling the wool over our eyes? The companies themselves become major things that we are ultimately lucky to be associated with. A clever trick indeed. If these states of mind and actions are not displaying the exact conditions necessary to be slavery according to the definition, then I will eat my hat. Wait, but there is more. Here is another section of Willie Lynches Letter.

Regarding information/knowledge (referred to as "language")

"...You know language is a peculiar institution. It leads to the heart of the people. The more a foreigner knows about the language of another country the more he is able to move through all levels of that society. Therefore, if the foreigner is an enemy of the country, to the extent that he knows the body of language, to that extent is the country vulnerable to attack or invasion of a foreign culture. For example, if you take a slave, if you teach him all about your language, he will know all your secrets, and he is then no more a slave, for you can't fool him any longer. For example, if you told a slave that he must perform in getting out "our crops" and he knows the language well, he would know that "our crops" didn't mean "our crops" and the slavery system would break down, for he would relate on the basis of what "our crops" really meant. So you have to be careful in setting up the new language for the slaves would soon be in your house, talking to you "man to man" and that is the death of our economic system."

The information/knowledge as it relates to today's' society is in part what I am providing here in this book. What traditional thought fails to realize about the institution of slavery as it existed in America is that it was an economic institution. Willie Lynch reiterates this in his speech when keeps referencing "their economic system." There is very little difference economically between big business today and major slave owners during the time of slavery. As it was vital for slave owners to control the mindsets of the slave population during slavery, is the case today for corporations to control the mindsets of the employee population. In the pages that follow, I will "spill the beans" so-to-speak on some information/knowledge that those advocating for big business would rather I not. For now, I want you to see and understand the complexity and cleverness of what Willie Lynch was teaching slave owners as well as how his message resonates (maybe even to a higher degree) in today's' capitalistic economy. Here is one last insert from his speeches that drives his message home even further.

Continuing discussion on information/knowledge

"...For example, if you put a slave in a hog pen and train him to live there and incorporate in him to value it as a way of life completely, the biggest problem you would have out of him is that he would worry you about provisions to keep the hog pen clean, or the same hog pen and make a slip and incorporate something in his language whereby he comes to value a house more than he does his hog pen, you got a problem. He will soon be in your house.

This last insert is particularly astounding as it relates strongly to what this book is about. In order to be a loser who wins, you need to know that other people and entities are present that stand to benefit socioeconomically by you failing to succeed. They would rather you focus on what you are being provided. Information and knowledge are being withheld so that you will not become aware of what it is that you do not have. They do not want you to even have an idea of the things that they themselves have. They especially don't want you to know and understand how you, through your own efforts, can obtain these things without them even being in the equation. They don't want you in a house. It is much better for them that you remain in your hog pen and to simply ask for better provisions. How about a $1.00 raise? Can I get a few more days off? What about some help with childcare? We will talk about it they say. Maybe we can come to a compromise, they agree. A give and a take will work just fine, they conclude. Meanwhile, you stay in your hog pen right where they want you to be. You are unaware of the nice houses that they live in. No, you are even unaware of the fact that they even exist. You work for Company X remember? You know, the job that your life and those you care about depend on. The one that you unquestionably work for as a dare I say, slave. Let's bring more light to what is going on in today's' capitalistic society.

Will The Real Hard Working People Please Stand Up

Ever notice how people in our society seem to be infatuated with being hardworking? I have no quarrels with being a hard worker. In fact, I submit that a bit of hard work will be necessary for you to be a loser that wins. What strikes me about the way that people in society use the words hard working is the context that it is being used. It first seems to be used as a differentiator between the "others" who I suppose don't work hard. This, in my view, is an unnecessary source of division, but more importantly, it seems to be used by society's members to indicate those that have jobs. Some consider it honorable to work 12-16 hour days or better still to work multiple jobs. After reading the last section, you are familiar with my ideas about unquestionably working for businesses (business owners) today. What I would like to discuss here is the origin of the concept of hard work that has people compelled to insist on doing it even if they, say, win the lottery. I'm fairly certain we have all heard of someone make such idiotic claims to continue working their $12.00 an hour job even if they won the $120 million dollar jackpot. Let's do a bit of math. At $12 an hour working 40 hours a week for say, 40 years, you'd stand to earn right at a whopping million dollars in gross wages. Not bad at all huh? Not bad, but if someone wins $120 million and they insist on spending that much of their lives in order to make a single million dollars, they are not using logical or even common sense. You all know the saying, "where there is smoke there is usually fire"? Well, there appears to be a lot of smoke in regards to the claim of hard work and this one seems to have societal influences written all over it.

In order to find the origin of our society's love affair with being such hard workers and contributing so much to other peoples' fortune, we have to go back to a period called the Gilded Age. It took place around the end of the 19th century, roughly from 1870-1900. It was a point in US history when industry began to boom. From railroad companies that emerged to fill the enormous need presented by the expansion to the western parts of the United States, to the growth of major industries like steel, jobs were aplenty. The changes in industries presented people of all kinds from foreign immigrants to southern blacks, with new opportunities to make a better living for themselves. Wages for skilled workers saw a major increase during the period. It was also the period where the people who owned the businesses became larger, more powerful, and wealthier than any had been able to prior to the period. So to summarize the period, you have a large number of people coming from far and wide to begin working for major industry on one hand, and on the other industry fat cats making more bank and gaining more power than had ever been had. Does anyone see any problems arising under these circumstances? It wouldn't take long before the workers, who were paid low wages and now dependent on the industries for their livelihoods, and the powerful industry owners to be at odds. The workers were upset by their working conditions which consisted of men, women, and children who would be required to work 12+ hour days, 6 days per week in working conditions that would be considered shady at best in regards to safety. The industry owners were focused on their bottom lines, of course, so they weren't obliged to see things from the workers' point of view. As a result, the workers banded together to form none other than what was referred to as the working class. Together they would fight against the fat cat industry owners in attempt to win better wages and working conditions. Many work unions emerged during this time period. They even presented political candidates for various offices including for the presidency of the United States.

What is most significant about the era is the emergence of the working class as a substantial group. Dependency on jobs instead of their own efforts in nature for people in society was now a thing. They had their own unions and political candidates. As with any substantial group in society, as they battled the powers that be of their time, I'm sure they developed quite a bit of pride along the way. They were the hard-working workers of the working class that made industry possible after all. They were going to voice their demands, and they deserved to be heard. This period in American History is essential to the change that occurred in the mindsets of the people in society. Prior to this period, Americans had a more direct relationship to the resources that they needed to live their lives. They had their own farms, small industries, and service businesses. When the Gilded Age took hold, a middle man became present between Americans and their resources. That middle man was Big Business, and it was a very powerful force indeed. That brings us to present day where not much has changed since then. Yes, the industrial revolution has ended and American Society looks a bit different since industry isn't as strong a force as it was back then. Yet, the exact same underlying principles remain. Big business still acts as an overwhelming middleman between society's members and the resources they need to survive. Big business owners are still primarily concerned about their bottom line. The working class of workers still have their pride in being hard workers. They have so much pride that it is a badge of honor to work obscene amounts of hours or have 2 or 3 different jobs that unapologetically infringe on their lives. So much pride does the hard worker have, that if provided with such luck to be able to financially provide for themselves and their families many times over, they would still never abandon their places as one of society's hard workers.

Corporations as People

Technically it isn't wrong for us in society to view employment as working for the company instead of the person or people who own the company. The reason is that our government provides the rights of people to our corporations. Yes, corporations in the United States are considered people just like you and I are. Corporations even have their own type of social security number. Some would say that these "people" have it better than the blood and bone people of our society. They certainly have better tax arrangements than we do. I'm not arguing against it, I'm merely stating that in our society the mighty corporation is king. Hear it roar! As people in society that harness so much economic power, let's take a look at how we, the actual people, do when compared to our fellow enterprising citizens.

Wages v/s Cost of Living

The median household income in the United States, as of August 2015, was $56,516 according to data from the U.S. Census. However, income varies according to our ages. Check out this 2017 salary data from the Bureau of Labor Statistics.

- 16 to 19 years: $422 weekly/$21,944 annually
- 20 to 24 years: $525 weekly/$27,300 annually
- 25 to 34 years: $776 weekly/$40,352 annually
- 35 to 44 years: $976 weekly/$50,752 annually
- 45 to 54 years: $975 weekly/$50,700 annually
- 55 to 64 years: $966 years/$50,232 annually
- 65 years and older: $904 weekly/$47,008 annually

These numbers would become extremely varied if we considered the region, sex, race, etc. Our focus is on the average. It appears that American salaries peak when they are between the ages of 35 to 44 at approximately $50,752. This is a major benchmark as it signifies the collective consensus of what our capitalist society with all of its corporations sees as fitting for an annual salary.

This number alone is completely arbitrary. I mean it all boils down to what you owe right? It's not how much money you make, but how much money you keep! To figure out how much money American's keep will take a look at the cost of living. Essentially, how much does food, shelter, clothing, household items, transportation, oh and let's not forget about adequate savings costs us? When you factor in that a large part of these costs are associated with corporations as they supply us with many of the things we need to live in today's society, it makes perfect sense to measure how they are treating us this way. Are they providing us with enough income from salaries to purchase the goods and services we need with plenty left over for savings and a few nonessentials? Wait! I forgot something. A huge factor that we must consider before we can even begin to count the beans to determine how we are making it. That huge factor is none other than Uncle Sam. Corporations do not concern themselves with the amount of taxes you have to pay on your salary nor do they factor in taxes when considering the price of the goods they sell us. Yet, we all have to pay taxes. In fact, the employee sees the highest income tax rates than any other earning group in our economy. An average of the progressive tax rates comes to 22.86%. The government does provide a tax allowance that varies according to each persons' situation, which is great since 22.86% on the $50,752 would leave us with only $39,657 net income after taxes. For now, we will not focus on the ramifications of taxes. Just keep in mind that sales and income taxes are very much alive and well in our society.

So just what is the cost of living in America? Thing is, the answer to this question is not cut and dry. There are too many variables to determine a single number that determines how much it cost to live in America. Cost of rent is generally going to be higher in the city than in the country. Some people or environments will need vehicles, whereas others will not need their own vehicle or they could use public transportation. The variables go on and on. However, there is a way to come to a good guess as to what the average cost of living is in America.

The average consumer unit in America spends about $60,060. This is a fancy way of saying the average household expenditure. Well, if you think back to what the average household income is ($56,516) you will see that we are already approximately $3,500 over budget. Still, let's take it a step further. The average US household has 2.53 members. We can use this number to determine what each member spends in a year according to the household numbers. It comes to about $23,739 for each person to live in America for a full year. At first glance, our average salary isn't fairing too bad. Even if you were to account for taxes, we'd still have some money left over to cover savings and some extremities. However, unless households suddenly all became single-member in the United States, there is more to this story.

We have to factor in our children and our spouses. Children don't generally work and are dependent. That means with one child or spouse that doesn't work, the living expense becomes about $47,500. Now things don't look so good. A family of three with one parent working and the other not would need $71,217 to live off of for the year. Let's also remember that our $56k salary was an average. Half will make more and half will make less, so there is no guarantee that the people in our example family of 3 are making even that. I encourage you to look at these figures and compare them to what you see in your economic environment. Are corporations providing United States citizens, whom they employ, enough to get by from your vantage point? From my vantage point, it has been no most of the time and barely when the answer has been yes. In many situations, people are working in households but still do not earn enough money through their incomes to live off of for the year without the assistance of government aid. I have rarely come into account of scenarios where people live in abundance. I would wager that this has been the case with you as well. According to the numbers as well as life experiences, I would say that our fellow corporate citizens get a grade of a huge capital F for Fail.

Some of you may be wondering why it is that our corporations fail us. Well, the answer is simple. Corporations are not created to take care of us. They are created to take care of a select few individuals. Its owners. The CEO of corporations are in essence the brain of the corporation and his main job is to increase value for the shareholders. That's it! Their jobs are not to increase the number of employees or to increase employee salary. It is to make the shareholders happy and that usually comes down to profits and performance in the marketplace. A system will almost always fail at a goal it was not designed to accomplish. In this case, the corporation was designed for the economic advancement of those who own it and not those who work for it.

Larry Gunter

Time as Money?

Which is more valuable time or money? For most the obvious answer is time, right? Well, that is unless you have no money. Then things are a bit different. There is a great philosopher that once said: "money isn't everything, but not having it is." That great philosopher is none other than Kanye West. Sarcasm aside, Kanye hit the nail on the head with this one. If you don't have any or enough money to live in this country then obtaining money is everything to you. When lack of money becomes an issue of life and death, it will always triumph over time. However, this is an extreme case. For most of us, we can agree that time is way more valuable to us than money. If this is true for most of us, as just stated, then the next obvious question in relation to the question of time and money is just how much money is time worth? Well, let's look at the highest average income again. We will ignore the fact that average salaries varied according to age. We will be very liberal in our assessment by assuming that we earned the highest average for the entirety of our careers working for ABC Corporation. We will also assume that ABC Corporation provides us with steady unflinching work for 43 years. That is we, graduated college at 22 years of age and worked there until we retired at 65 years old. At retirement, we would have earned about $2,182,336 working for ABC Corporation. The question is whether or not this is enough to pay for the time we spent there. There is also a cost to effort and knowledge, but we will leave those out to keep things simple. So let's see, working 40 hours a week for 52 weeks comes to 2,080 hours a year. Now all that we need to do is multiply our work hours each year by the 43 years we spent working at ABC Corporation. This comes to 89,440 hours. Wow! That's a lot of the hours! In fact with the current life expectancy in the United States at 78 years, we would've spent a whopping 13.1% of our lives dedicated to ABC Corporation. Considering that we spend about 1/3 of our lives sleeping, let's look at the percentage of time we would spend working at ABC Corporation from our awake time. About 19.6% of our time would be dedicated to ABC Corporation. Wow! That's a lot! It's essentially 1 out of every 5 hours that we would spend awake. I'm not saying whether it's a good thing or a bad thing per se. I'm merely stating that it is very significant and as valuable as life hours actually are, I'm wondering if the $2,182,336 over 43 years is enough. We know that at the micro-level it's $24.40 for each one of those hours. According to these figures, let's determine just how much society and its corporations are essentially telling us our lives are worth. They say that our lives at $24.40 an hour are worth $16,672,032. How about just our awake hours? They tell us that also at $24.40 an hour the hours we are awake in our lives total $11,114,688.

These figures by no means tell us what our lives are financially worth. That is for each one of us to decide for ourselves. However, whether we realize it or not, it is what society and its corporations are telling us. This is how much they are willing to pay us for those hours that we have a finite amount of. These are hours that we cannot be with our loved ones, visiting the world, or simply staying at home reading a book. In the end, they are all that we have as they end up being the accumulation of what our lives were. Whether you think $16 million or $11 million for awake hours are enough is entirely your call. I only bring up the point to emphasize that the hours we have are very valuable. They shouldn't be so readily given away without seriously considering their worth as well as how much we are selling them for. What would you do with that $24.40? What could you do with that hour? Think long and hard about it. This decision only accounts for 10.2 valuable years of your life.

Your World Is Yours

In this chapter, my goal was to drive home the idea that you should not be forced to compromise how you spend your time living in this world. In your efforts to win, you have already lost if you fall prey to the outside gravitational pull against your hours. You are truly a valuable resource. There are many in this world who know this all too well. It is about time that you realize this and commit to expending your time and efforts on your terms. As we saw in Willie Lynches' speech and continue to see as our current economic systems echo his words in practice, keeping knowledge hidden from us is a big deal. The last thing they want is for us to be showing up in their houses acting as though we belong. I'm speaking figuratively of course. In order to win, you will need to make it a point to learn the "language" or knowledge that they want to remain hidden. You will need to abandon the ideals that society has grabbed hold of over the years that keep a significant number of its members from advancing like the notion of a "hard worker". There are many cultural themes behind such mindsets that are the equivalent of chains on our hands and feet keeping us from realizing real upward mobility. You must also carefully analyze what corporations are. How they function and what their goals truly are. They are not built to provide for you and your family. That is what you were built for and no other person or entity can do it better than you can. Always think about and consider the value of your time. It is in my opinion that the most valuable nonrenewable resource that the world has ever known is the hour of a person. All too often, those that seek it know its worth, while those that actually harness it give it away so freely. This will never be a winning scenario for those seeking to win.

Once we make our minds up to control our own destinies, we will be able to realize that the odds are in our favor. In the next chapter, I will be bringing light to a vital piece of "language" that will complete your journey of realizing what it takes to become a winner. It is no less than the economic Holy Grail! You have rejected the notion of becoming one of society's winners. You have become mentally free and found out who you actually are. Just now you have realized the value of your hours and how essential it is that you are the one in control of them. Now, you will find out how to empower yourself in our society using the tools it so readily provides. Now it is time to talk about business with a capital B.

CHAPTER 5:

Rich Business, Poor Business

"I'd rather have 1 percent of the efforts of 100 people than 100 percent of my own efforts."

- *Jean Paul Getty*

Business Owners Win

I am not going to beat around the bush here. If you want to win, building your own business or businesses is the key. This is the common factor that all of the losers who won had. They, in some shape form or fashion, took the initiative to be the controller and operator of their own endeavors. It didn't matter if they had a product to sell or if they themselves were the product. They all owned their own businesses. Look at the wording here. Business owners. Owning your own business. Hmm, so what is business again? I am so glad you asked, as I have an answer to that question.

Business: A person's regular occupation, profession, or trade

In other words, your business is what you do for a living. You either have control as the owner or someone one else does. I'm telling you here and now that you should always own that. Doesn't matter if you make art, are a fisherman, truck driver, accountant, customer service rep, hardwood floor installer, financial analyst, law enforcer, or video gamer. As a loser who wants to win, owning your own business is the key to you being absolutely free. You see, when it comes down to it, that is what this book is all about. Once you remove the chains on your mind to become socially free and activate the skills necessary to be economically free, you are undoubtedly winning! It doesn't matter what your background is or your current circumstances. Everyone is able to free their own minds, discover themselves, and own their own businesses. In our society, it is when we seek to sell our business to others that limitations are present. Furthermore, if we seek to own our business ourselves, our society has open doors just waiting for us to walk through them. The problem is these doors are not out in the open for us to see. They don't teach about these doors in schools. Society is too busy teaching us to be winners. That is to adhere to the brainwashing of the matrix and to sell your business to the highest bidder that you can find. You see, our society is not very interested in your social and economic freedom. I would go so far as to say that it has an invested interest in you not being socially and economically free. Society will work better having it that way. There is nothing wrong with that. It is the function of society, and as I stated earlier society has its place and does good work. It keeps us safe and makes the world we live in easier to navigate by simplifying thought and processes. However, if you are made of a different fabric from those who follow and advocate for society's control, then you must reject its messages and its contracts. You must always reject society's winner strategy consisting of selling your business. Here is more on what it means and looks like for you to own your business.

Is it Your Job or Your Business?

Many people have the wrong idea in regards to what it means to own their own business. If you are not careful, you could find yourself thinking you are the owner of your own business when in fact all that you are owning is your own job. Aren't they the same thing, you may ask? Well not exactly. If you own your business it is true that you own your own job as well. However, if you just own your own job that means someone else still owns your business. At the end of the day when it comes to this distinction, it all comes down to control. Who is in control of your job and your income? In other words, if you decided not to do anything for a specific week, would your occupational circumstance have the potential to change? Notice I did not mention would your money change. You may be in a situation where your business requires your effort for 100% of your income. In this case, if you took a week off to go to Hawaii you wouldn't make any income that week. However, it still is your business if once you return from your trip, you have no concerns on whether you still have your job. If there is no other entity present that can make a decision against your job, chances are you own your business. On the other hand, if you return from your vacation and there is a person or entity that can make a decision to decrease or do away with your job, then you simply own your job. There are a lot of independent contractor arrangements set up this way. I know this because I have been in such situations many times before. I was not in full control of my job. Not all independent contractor situations are like mine. There are plenty of circumstances out there where having independent contracts create business ownership for the contractor. I have mentioned my experiences to highlight the important distinction between owning your own business and owning your job.

I-N-C. For You and Me

When you think of a corporation what comes to mind? For many of us, it's a huge firm with board members and a home office high rise building to handle the administrative work for its thousands of employees. This was my subconscious view of a corporation for a very long time. Although the above idea of a corporation is not necessarily false, it most definitely isn't all that a corporation can be. The truth is that a corporation can be as big as a large company like Walmart that is traded on the stock market and has locations throughout the world, or it could be a single mother working out of her home selling a few knits a month at her local flea market. Walmart is no more of a corporation than her business is if she has filed to incorporate with the government. There are no special qualifications of money or scale required for a company to run as an official corporation. This is such an important point that I am going to burn a few more lines to restate it again. There are no special qualifications of money or scale required for a company to run as an official corporation. Ok so let me take it a bit further. There are also no special qualifications of money or status required for an individual to start a corporation. Let's repeat this groundbreaking detail as well. There are also no special qualifications of money or status required for an individual to start a corporation. All that is required for a business to become a corporation is to file with a state. It could be the state that you live in, but it most certainly does not have to be. Once you have filed with the state in which you choose, your business would have become just as much a corporation as Walmart is. More on why this is so important later. For now, here is a list of all US states and their fees associated with forming and maintaining a corporation as of 2016. Included are the required fees to start an LLC as well. LLC's are also considered to be corporations.

1. **Alabama:**
    a. LLC
        i. Filing Fee:$165
        ii. Annual Report:$0
    b. Incorporation
        i. Filing Fee:$165
        ii. Annual Report:$0
2. **Alaska:**
    a. LLC
        i. Filing Fee:$250

        ii. Initial Report:$0
        iii. Annual Report:$100
    b. Incorporation
        i. Filing Fee:$250
        ii. Initial Report:$0
        iii. Annual Report:$100
3. **Arizona**
    a. LLC
        i. Filing Fee:$50
        ii. Publication Fee:$299
        iii. Annual Report:$0
    b. Incorporation
        i. Filing Fee:$60
        ii. Publication Fee:$299
        iii. Annual Report:$45
4. **Arkansas**
    a. LLC
        i. Filing Fee:$50
        ii. Annual Report:$150
    b. Incorporation
        i. Filing Fee:$50
        ii. Annual Report:$150
5. **California**
    a. LLC
        i. Filing Fee:$75
        ii. Initial Report:$20
        iii. Annual Report:$20
    b. Incorporation
        i. Filing Fee:$105
        ii. Initial Report:$25
        iii. Annual Report:$25
6. **Colorado**
    a. LLC
        i. Filing Fee:$50
        ii. Annual Report:$10
    b. Incorporation
        i. Filing Fee:$50
        ii. Annual Report:$10
7. **Connecticut**
    a. LLC
        i. Filing Fee:$175
        ii. Annual Report:$25
    b. Incorporation
        i. Filing Fee:$455
        ii. Annual Report:$100

8. **District of Columbia**
   a. LLC
      i. Filing Fee:$220
      ii. Annual Report:$300
   b. Incorporation
      i. Filing Fee:$220
      ii. Annual Report:$300
9. **Delaware:**
   a. LLC
      i. Filing Fee:$140
      ii. Annual report:$300
   b. Incorporation
      i. Filing Fee:$140
      ii. Annual Report:$225(minimum)
10. **Florida**
    a. LLC
       i. Filing Fee:$155
       ii. Annual Report:$138.75
    b. Incorporation
       i. Filing Fee:$78.75
       ii. Annual Report:$150
11. **Georgia**
    a. LLC
       i. Filing Fee:$100
       ii. Annual Report:$50
    b. Incorporation
       i. Filing Fee:$100
       ii. Publication Fee:$150
       iii. Initial Report:$50
       iv. Annual Report:$50
12. **Hawaii**
    a. LLC
       i. Filing Fee:$50
       ii. Annual Report:$15
    b. Incorporation
       i. Filing Fee:$50
       ii. Annual Report:$15
13. **Idaho**
    a. LLC
       i. Filing Fee:$100
       ii. Annual Report:$0
    b. Incorporation
       i. Filing Fee:$101
       ii. Annual Report:$0
14. **Illinois**

a. LLC
    i. Filing Fee:$500
    ii. Annual Report:$305
b. Incorporation
    i. Filing Fee:$175
    ii. Annual Report:$155

15. **Indiana**
a. LLC
    i. Filing Fee:$90
    ii. Annual Report:$30
b. Incorporation
    i. Filing Fee:$90
    ii. Annual Report:$30

16. **Iowa**
a. LLC
    i. Filing Fee:$50
    ii. Annual Report:$45
b. Incorporation
    i. Filing Fee:$50j
    ii. Annual Report:$45

17. **Kansas**
a. LLC
    i. Filing Fee:$160
    ii. Annual Report:$55
b. Incorporation
    i. Filing Fee:$90
    ii. Annual Report:$55

18. **Kentucky**
a. LLC
    i. Filing Fee:$55
    ii. Annual Fee:$15
b. Incorporation
    i. Filing Fee:$55
    ii. Annual Report:$15

19. **Louisiana**
a. LLC
    i. Filing Fee:$100
    ii. Annual Report:$30
b. Incorporation
    i. Filing Fee:$100
    ii. Annual Report:$30

20. **Maine**
a. LLC
    i. Filing Fee:$175
    ii. Annual Report:$85

        b. Incorporation
            i. Filing Fee:$145
            ii. Annual Report:$85

21. **Maryland**
        a. LLC
            i. Filing Fee:$155
            ii. Annual Report:$300 (minimum)
        b. Incorporation
            i. Filing Fee:$155
            ii. Annual Report:$300 (minimum)

22. **Massachusetts**
        a. LLC
            i. Filing Fee:$520
            ii. Annual Report:$520
        b. Incorporation
            i. Filing Fee:$295
            ii. Annual Report:$135

23. **Michigan**
        a. LLC
            i. Filing Fee:$50
            ii. Annual Report:$25
        b. Incorporation
            i. Filing Fee:$60
            ii. Annual Report:$25

24. **Minnesota**
        a. LLC
            i. Filing Fee:$160
            ii. Annual Report:$0
        b. Incorporation
            i. Filing Fee:$160
            ii. Annual Report:$0

25. **Mississippi**
        a. LLC
            i. Filing Fee:$50
            ii. Annual Report:$25
        b. Incorporation
            i. Filing Fee:$50
            ii. Annual Report:$25

26. **Missouri**
        a. LLC
            i. Filing Fee:$50
            ii. Annual Report:$0
        b. Incorporation
            i. Filing Fee:$58
            ii. Initial Report:$45

iii. Annual Report:$45

27. **Montana**
    a. LLC
       i. Filing Fee:$70
       ii. Annual Report:$15
    b. Incorporation
       i. Filing Fee:$70
       ii. Annual Report:$15

28. **Nebraska**
    a. LLC
       i. Filing Fee:$120
       ii. Publication Fee:$150
       iii. Annual Report:$26
    b. Incorporation
       i. Filing Fee:$65
       ii. Publication Fee:$150
       iii. Annual Report:$26

29. **Nevada**
    a. LLC
       i. Filing Fee:$75
       ii. Initial Report:$325
       iii. Annual Report:$325
    b. Incorporation
       i. Filing Fee:$75
       ii. Initial Report:$325
       iii. Annual Report:$325

30. **New Hampshire**
    a. LLC
       i. Filing Fee:$100
       ii. Annual Report:$100
    b. Incorporation
       i. Filing Fee:$100
       ii. Annual Report:$100

31. **New Jersey**
    a. LLC
       i. Filing Fee:$125
       ii. Annual Report:$50
    b. Incorporation
       i. Filing Fee:$125
       ii. Annual Report:$50

32. **New Mexico**
    a. LLC
       i. Filing Fee:$50
       ii. Annual Report:$0
    b. Incorporation

               i. Filing Fee:$100
               ii. Initial Report:$25
               iii. Annual Report:$25

33. **New York**
    a. LLC
        i. Filing Fee:$210
        ii. Annual Report:$9
        iii. Publication Fee:$425-$1200
    b. Incorporation
        i. Filing Fee:$145
        ii. Annual Report:$9

34. **North Carolina**
    a. LLC
        i. Filing Fee:$125
        ii. Annual Report:$202
    b. Incorporation
        i. Filing Fee:$125
        ii. Annual Report:$20

35. **North Dakota**
    a. LLC
        i. Filing Fee:$135
        ii. Annual Report:$50
    b. Incorporation
        i. Filing Fee:$100
        ii. Annual Report:$25

36. **Ohio**
    a. LLC
        i. Filing Fee:$125
        ii. Annual Report:$0
    b. Incorporation
        i. Filing Fee:$125
        ii. Annual Report:$0

37. **Oklahoma**
    a. LLC
        i. Filing Fee:$104
        ii. Annual Report:$25
    b. Incorporation
        i. Filing Fee:$52
        ii. Annual Report:$0

38. **Oregon**
    a. LLC
        i. Filing Fee:$100
        ii. Annual Report:$100
    b. Incorporation
        i. Filing Fee:$100

ii. Annual Report:$100

39. **Pennsylvania**
   a. LLC
      i. Filing Fee:$125
      ii. Annual Report:$0
   b. Incorporation
      i. Filing Fee:$125
      ii. Annual Report:$0
      iii. Publication Fee:$299

40. **Rhode Island**
   a. LLC
      i. Filing Fee:$150
      ii. Annual Report:$50
   b. Incorporation
      i. Filing Fee:$230
      ii. Annual Report:$50

41. **South Carolina**
   a. LLC
      i. Filing Fee:$110
      ii. Annual Report:$0
   b. Incorporation
      i. Filing Fee:$135
      ii. Annual Report:$0
      iii. Attorney Signature Fee:$100

42. **South Dakota**
   a. LLC
      i. Filing Fee:$150
      ii. Annual Report:$50
   b. Incorporation
      i. Filing Fee:$150
      ii. Annual Report:$50

43. **Tennessee**
   a. LLC
      i. Filing Fee:$325
      ii. Annual Report:$310
   b. Incorporation
      i. Filing Fee:$125
      ii. Annual Report:$20

44. **Texas**
   a. LLC
      i. Filing Fee:$310
      ii. Annual Report: (Depends on gross annual revenue)
   b. Incorporation
      i. Filing Fee:$310

ii. Annual Report: (Depends on gross annual revenue)

45. **Utah**
    a. LLC
        i. Filing Fee:$72
        ii. Annual Report:$15
    b. Incorporation
        i. Filing Fee:$72
        ii. Annual Report:$15

46. **Vermont**
    a. LLC
        i. Filing Fee:$125
        ii. Annual Report:$25
    b. Incorporation
        i. Filing Fee:$125
        ii. Annual Report:$35

47. **Virginia**
    a. LLC
        i. Filing Fee:$104
        ii. Annual Report:$50
    b. Incorporation
        i. Filing Fee:$79
        ii. Annual Report:$100

48. **Washington**
    a. LLC
        i. Filing Fee:$200
        ii. Initial Report:$10
        iii. Annual Report:$73
    b. Incorporation
        i. Filing Fee:$200
        ii. Initial Report:$10
        iii. Annual Report:$73

49. **West Virginia**
    a. LLC
        i. Filing Fee:$132
        ii. Annual Report:$25
    b. Incorporation
        i. Filing Fee:$82
        ii. Annual Report:$25

50. **Wisconsin**
    a. LLC
        i. Filing Fee:$130
        ii. Annual Report:$25
    b. Incorporation
        i. Filing Fee:$100

ii. Annual Report:$40
51. **Wyoming**
    a. LLC
        i. Filing Fee:$103
        ii. Annual Report:$52
    b. Incorporation
        i. Filing Fee:$103
        ii. Annual Report:$52

Liability & Taxes

When it comes to owning your own business by forming a corporation it is important to remember one very important concept. We discussed this concept in the last chapter in fact. The concept is that corporations are considered to be people. Ok, so what that means is the exact same benefits that large corporations like Walmart enjoy, so can you in your businesses. This puts a tremendous amount of power in the hands of the people. American society is a capitalistic society. This is why there are many tools and advantages present to help the capitalists within it to be successful. In our economic system, every single person has the ability to create their own version of powerful entities like McDonald's. As long as we are able to pay the fees and submit the appropriate paperwork, we can create economic entities that are treated as separate people from us.

There are several reasons why the ability to form corporations in our society is so important to us individuals who are looking to win. Let us consider the concept of liability. Imagine that you, using a $25,000 personal loan formed a business that is not incorporated. You spend $20,000 to buy supplies and equipment and hire an employee to do the work. On the first day, what if your employee has an accident that causes $50,000 in damages. Your business would be in serious trouble before it even gets off the ground good. It is now not only responsible for the $20,000 spent on supplies and equipment, but it is now being sued for $50,000. All that you have in the businesses bank account is the $5,000. Let's say you decide it is time to cut your losses. Clearly, luck is not on your side if such a terrible thing would happen on your business's very first day. Well, you pay the remaining $5,000 of the $75,000 bill and now your business owes $70,000. What is your business to do? You just folded so there will be no revenues coming in, yet this huge bill remains. Give up? The answer is, nothing. There is absolutely nothing that your business can do. It has done all that it can by paying all its remaining money towards its liabilities. However, this is not the end of this story. Because you did not send in your documents and pay your fees with the state to incorporate your business, you as the business owner are now responsible for the remaining debt. In court proceedings a judge can order you to pay the debt out of the money you hold in your personal checking/savings, money you have in a retirement fund, any stock or mutual funds you may have, or any other thing of value that could be appraised and applied towards the debt that you personally owe. Even your property such as your family home can be taken from you and sold in order to satisfy your debt. Why? Simply because you did not have any liability protection between you and your business. If you had formed an LLC or a corporation there would be a barrier between you and your business protecting you from the liability your employee created. Your business would still have been ordered by a judge to pay what is owed, but since it was operating as a person in the view of society and business law, it would be solely responsible for the expenses. Your personal assets would be 100 percent safe. It doesn't matter if you have only 1 business incorporated or 100 incorporated businesses, all that you could lose if your businesses end up owing debt is the money or assets you put into the business. What I have just outlined is one of the many powers of incorporating, and why you should always incorporate if you want to win!

Now let's consider taxes. People who are classified as employees or self-employed receive the highest tax rates. In our capitalist society, there have been many changes to the tax laws that are advantageous to incorporated businesses. Society wants its corporations to succeed and employ members of society remember. It needs to have striving businesses all over to employ all the winners it manufactures. Well, as an owner of an LLC or a Corporation guess what? You get to take advantage of all of these tax advantages. That means that you and your little incorporated lemonade stand is obligated to the same tax benefits as Walmart. As a loser looking to win, you'd only be hurting yourself if you failed to take advantage of it. The specific advantages that you and your incorporated business can receive are subjective to your business and its performance. However, there are four advantages worth noting here.

Benefit Deductions: Incorporated businesses have the ability to deduct so-called fringe benefits. This includes daily business and travel expenses as well as expenses such as medical insurance. Your own income tax also has the potential to be lower as incorporated business enterprises are taxed at a lower rate.

Deducting Losses: If your business isn't financially successful you can deduct the losses in your income taxes. Essentially, any losses that the business has can be used to decrease your overall tax liability.

Business Items: The cost of the equipment that your business needs to function can be used as tax deductions. This goes for anything from vehicles and associated expenses to computer hardware and software.

Social Security Tax Deduction: Social security taxes for employees and self-employed classified workers are very substantial expenses that are deducted from all of the money you earn. If you own an incorporated business, however, you have the ability to classify business income in categories other than salary or personal income. This means that you may not be required to pay social security taxes on 100% of the income earned which is a huge perk.

I am no tax law expert. Do not consider the above information to be tax advice. You should consult with an actual accountant or trusted advisor in matters of taxation concerning your business. Just be sure to take note that tax advantages are out there for you and your incorporated businesses to use. These advantages are put in place so that your incorporated businesses will have a better chance of being successful and employing society's winners. They just happen to also be there to help losers like you and I win.

Drumroll Please...

This next section contains some of the most powerful words in this entire book. This section contains a game-changer that Willie Lynch himself would go through great lengths to keep from you. This is the sort of "language" that will have you in his house for sure! What I am about to share has the power to set you and every single member of your family up to be financially free for the rest of your lives. It is just that powerful! If used to maximum effect, you will never feel financially pressured to sell your business to another entity ever again. This will be the case even if you aren't fortunate enough to have successful businesses over many years. To put it another way, you can start several incorporated businesses that fail over many years and never want for a single thing along the way. Society through its' capitalistic ideals and business laws make it so. This may be the reason that what I am about to share with you isn't shouted from rooftop to rooftop, or in todays' time, tweeted from coast to coast. It's one of our society's best-kept secrets, and I am about to share it with you in this section of this book. As I reveal this secret that isn't actually a secret at all, but rather a type of strategic tool, your journey should come to a full circle. My promise to you was that by the end of this book, I would provide you with the knowledge for you to win. This last piece of the puzzle will empower you and anyone you share the teachings in this book with to achieve the American Dream. I don't care if you are an upper manager of a firm, a recent college grad, a high school dropout, or were just released from prison, you will have the ability to move mountains for yourself and your loved ones. The truth of the matter is that we all have had the ability to adopt these mindsets and to use the strategy I am about to reveal for our entire adult lives. We have not done so for one simple reason. We were not taught to think this way. We were most certainly not taught to use the upcoming strategy. We were all in the dark. My fellow losers, I am honored to flip that light switch on for you all.

Let's start at the beginning. As a citizen of the United States, you are issued a number. This number has many uses. One of those uses is for creditors to identify you. They use your number to pull up your credit data so that they may make informed decisions of whether to issue you credit or not. Of course, this is not new news. You already knew that, right? Well, have you ever thought about business credit? I know that I didn't for a very long time. I subconsciously figured it was something big multimillion-dollar corporations used exclusively for major projects like building factories overseas. Boy was I wrong! I am not ashamed to admit it either. I didn't realize at the time how all incorporated businesses have the same rights and are thus treated the same on paper. What I mean by treated the same "on paper" is that government agencies, as well as any other commercial firms, must look at all incorporated businesses as entities themselves separate from any person's personal social security number. What this means is that just as the court honors the incorporated business as adequate enough itself to be 100 percent liable for any expenses that it incurs, so is the case with creditors providing credit. Let's dig deeper.

How many of you losers have a rich uncle handy that you can tell your latest and greatest idea to so that he can pull out the old checkbook and "F up some commas" on your behalf? I'm going to go out on a limb and say well over the majority of you do not. If only we did. We would have started several businesses by now. No doubt, many of them would be unsuccessful, but the idea is that eventually, we would have a win, right? If only we had a rich uncle or two. Well, I'm here to tell that you absolutely do not need one! None of you do!

The book *Rich Dad Poor Dad* by Robert Kiyosaki changed my life. If you have not read the book, I strongly encourage you to do so. The foundational principles of that book which the author applies to personal finance provides the basis for what I am advocating you all do with your own incorporated businesses. I will briefly state the major concepts here, but for a more in depth analysis, I encourage you to obtain a copy of the book and read it for yourself. There is one particular quote that is essential to the ideas I'm conveying. Here it is.

"Be careful when you take on debt. If you take on debt personally, make sure it is small. If you take on large debt, make sure someone else is paying for it."

-Robert Kiyosaki

I remember when I first began to think about this concept, it drove me nuts! I was extremely intrigued by the idea of leveraging personal credit in a way that I would not have to put up any cash to pay for my investments. In my mind, I could see it happening right before my eyes. I would go to the bank and finance pieces of property that were selling for lower than what they were worth. I'd then apply any sweat equity that was necessary to bring up the values of the properties to a price well above what I paid. Lastly, I'd either sell the properties for a huge net profit or I'd rent the properties for higher than the mortgages I had on the properties. There would be nothing left for me to do at that point but to collect the revenue derived from the difference. My tenants would be paying off the money I owed as well as paying me. I'd have debt, but it would be good debt, which is what the author of Rich Dad Poor Dad advocates!

I first read that book over 15 years ago. There are still principles in it that I live by to this day. However, I have evolved a bit since reading it when it comes to the subject matter of personal debt. I do not advise anyone to make it a habit of acquiring personal debt in an attempt to realize business gains. Though the author had the right idea about using other peoples' money, he was wrong to suggest using personal credit. In the economic system that we have all inherited, there is simply no reason for anyone to ever wager their personal assets for their business. The ability for anyone to easily start, own, and build credit for an incorporated business, while remaining personally protected is no less than the goose that lays the golden egg! Rich Dad Poor Dad's author got it wrong by failing to mention that we, as United States Citizens, have the ability to create corporate entities that we own which we can leverage to take on debt for us! I am really hoping this is all sinking in. None of us need rich uncles because we can simply create incorporated businesses, without any personal liability, that will provide the financing we need to start and run our businesses ourselves! If we want another one, two, or two hundred there is nothing in our society that will stop us. If we wanted to we could register the two hundred incorporated businesses with the state at the same time. We have that power and thus the power to control our own destinies. The power to be free.

I want to be perfectly clear before moving on. I insinuated that you and your family members would be able to avoid feeling the financial pressures of ever needing to sell your business. I have also emphasized how incorporated businesses are separate entities from its owners. So you may be wondering how it is that you and I can be financially free for years to come by obtaining credit for our incorporated businesses. The answer is rather simple. What is it that our businesses need to work? They will probably need equipment or supplies of some kind, but most importantly they are going to need human capital. Your incorporated business entities will need people to make it function and do things. How do businesses get people to work for them? They pay them of course. Your businesses will pay you for your work. The goal is for your businesses to generate income and to be completely dependent on revenues instead of credit for day to day operations. This includes using revenues to pay your salary. However, if your businesses aren't yet generating enough income itself to pay you then you have every right to get paid. The business can then use its credit to pay you for your work. This idea turns Rich Dad Poor Dad's theory on its end. Instead of other people paying your debt, here you have other people, taking on the risk for your business endeavors. These other people will be your business creditors. You will no doubt attempt to turn your incorporated businesses into major companies that provide a good service to the world. You will attempt to have it so that your businesses will provide those seeking to be winners in society with good jobs to work for the rest of their lives. Unfortunately, whatever your intent, this will not all ways be possible. Let's face it, businesses sometimes fail. You can do everything in your power to dot every "I" and to cross every "T", but it may still not be enough. If this happens and your business owes substantial debt from the business equipment and the salary you paid yourself to the extent that it can no longer function, you simply close the doors to that particular business. You will then take with you the lessons you learned from the experience on to your next incorporated business. Oh and guess what? Your incorporated business being its own standalone entity will be solely responsible for the loss that it incurred. In other words, even though you were receiving a salary for your work in the business, your personal assets will be off-limits to creditors who may come looking. This also goes for any dividends that you may have paid yourself from net profits had your business once been solvent enough to pay them.

Now I hope that you all are able to fully grasp the significance of what I have just shared with you. We all have the ability to change our worlds. We have always had this ability, but we simply were not aware. I encourage you to take a hard look at the costs associated with incorporating a business in your state or the states you plan to conduct your business in. These costs vary by state, but none of them are so significant that we wouldn't be able to come up with the fees in time. If you have the means and the desire to incorporate more than one business at one time, I say go for it. You can even pay yourself smaller amounts out of each incorporated business which would mean lower debt accumulation for each one. They would all simply share the burden of providing your salary. I then encourage you to work hard in your businesses to make your dreams come true! With this newfound information, you now have the power to make it happen for you and your family!

Rinse and Repeat

I sincerely want every last one of you losers to work hard and build your own incorporated businesses. No doubt that would mean that several of your businesses will not be successful. I am ok with that. If businesses fold and creditors end up not getting paid, I say it is a part of the business that they are in. They are in a business that involves a risk of losing their money.

They don't even refer to it as money that they would be losing. For them, it is actually called an investment. These businesses provide money to other businesses at an expense called interest. Therefore there is absolutely nothing wrong with using this leverage to fund our endeavors. However, what I do have a problem with is a fraud. I am by no means suggesting nor do I condone anyone taking this information and using it to take advantage of creditors. If you and your incorporated businesses take on business credit, you must be operating in good faith. That means you must have every intention of having a business that is successful, and repaying every single penny acquired from creditors. In fact, it is absolutely necessary that incorporated businesses conduct themselves as such in order for its owners to receive liability shields from financial and criminal charges. In the event that debt is owed, the owners of incorporated businesses will have the burden of providing substantial evidence that the business was in fact not just a shell for the owners' gain. If in a court of law it can be proved the owners used the incorporated business in such a way, they will be personally responsible for all damages.

Let me also state that acquiring business credit, just as is the case when acquiring personal credit, is a process. This process will take a bit of time and effort as business creditors have processes in place to minimize the risk of loss of their assets. My next project will be a manual entitled *How Losers Start Businesses: A step by step guide to incorporating your business and building business credit.* In this work, I will be providing an easy step by step guide that you can follow to get your businesses off the ground without trouble. This manual will provide you with a turnkey solution that has done all the leg work for you. It will provide you with all the answers you will need to incorporate and build business credit for your businesses.

CONCLUSION:

Now What?

"Freedom is never more than one generation away from extinction. We didn't pass it to our children in the bloodstream. It must be fought for, protected, and handed on for them to do the same."

\- *Ronald Reagan*

Philosophy Behind It All

W hether we like it or not, we are all a part of society. Seemingly at the moment of our conception, it began imprinting its mark on us. There is no doubt that it significantly contributed to making each one of us who we are today. There is absolutely no denying that. It provides us with many tools that we use every day in our lives. These tools make life easier and safer for us to navigate through as we soar across the planet elbow to elbow with millions of other complex minds. Because of society, we know the difference between a safe and unsafe environment. Because of society, when confronted with extreme circumstances, we know how to act appropriately. Society teaches us to rally behind one another when a great many of us are suffering such as the case of when a natural disaster hits. We know how to be content with what we ourselves have despite clear evidence laying right before us that others have much more. Society provides us with social, economic, and political governing entities that are constantly working behind the scenes to make sure we don't lose our collective sense of safety. Society with all its might and beauty manages to finesse its way in and throughout our lives simultaneously making each one of us feel that we are safe and that we belong. Society is good for us.

Yet, society is still not without issues and challenges. It

sometimes sends mixed messages and doesn't always work for greater prosperity for all. In fact, it very often works in a way that advocates for great prosperity for a select few at the expense of many others. Further, in order for society to work it oftentimes must alienate certain groups within it in order to ensure that the greater whole, is kept in line. I was driven to write this book on behalf of one of those alienated groups. Our beloved society would consider members of this group to be losers. Society is not welcoming to its losers. Society's losers present a serious threat to it. They are the equivalent of destructive computer viruses lurking in the shadows with the potential ability to take the whole system down. I myself am one of these losers. Most people, as loyal members of society, will see this book of mine, this subjectively valuable piece of work, as a strike against their existence. I am speaking of those who are committed to the concept of being one of society's winners. Thus, I cannot hold any rebukes of this work against them. They are all a part of it, you see. A part of this thing I referred to as the matrix. They are a part of the societal system which has a very important job of boldly and unapologetically rejecting everyone and everything that goes against the system.

Knowing that this book would be controversial, I still felt obligated to write it. You see, just because a thing is a virus only states that it seeks to infect a host. Neither the virus nor its host has any predetermined knowledge of whether the changes it would make to the program would be for the better or for the worse. I am obliged to believe that the concepts in this book if implemented would make society better. No this would not be the case if every single member read and subscribed the ideals and practices within. This book is intended for the relatively small group of people who, like its author, have been cast aside by society and its players. It is my belief that these people would better serve themselves and society if they embraced who they were and began the work of creating and innovating. This is what we are naturally calibrated to do.

I also feel as though society is fully aware of our existence and realizes the great work that we can do to improve on its systems. This is the reason that it has provided us with such magnificent tools to do our work with. Deep down society wants us to embrace our true selves and abandon the messages that it presents to all of its winners and potentials. It never intends to infiltrate our minds with its mass messages. It wants us to be socially and economically free, but it can never let that be known. It would then lose every single bit of its credibility. Society has created a social order that must include a message of limitation. It infects the majority of its members and uses each individuals' social tools to influence people in their relatively small social circles. One person seems insignificant, but society knows that by activating a few people here and there, it won't take long before virtually everyone is affected. Each person within distinct social groups, unknowingly submitting to the same ideals, work together to push its great plan. On the other hand, society has an economic system that works a totally different way altogether. It is all-inclusive and empowers everyone. It truly advocates for everyone to be free. There are no barriers to entry nor gatekeepers keeping members of society from taking advantage of all that it has to offer. However, unlike society's social system, it lacks any significant way of spreading the word. In fact, if everyone finds out how it works and decided to take advantage of it all at the same time it would fall apart. The economic system is more fragile and less equipped for the masses to collectively plunder. So at the end of the day society has built these two systems in ways that seem odd, but ultimately makes sense. It has created a social system for the masses which provides the illusion of total freedom when in reality its members aren't mentally free at all. At the same time, it has created an economic system that provides the illusion to the masses of strict rules, insurmountable boundaries, and barriers to entry when in reality any and all of society's members have the power and ability to take full advantage of its benefits with little to no resistance. How ironic!

Knowledge Is Power

I am absolutely thrilled that you read this book! I have this vision of each and every person that reads this book becoming super motivated and right then and there going out to change their circumstances. If you are indeed a loser like me then I know that you were built to go against the grain and do just that. I can only hope that this book has provided you with enough insight and inspiration to embrace who you are. The influencers of the world hold too much power. It does our world a great disservice when people like yourself, whom I believe are more capable than any to do great things, are demotivated and told to take a back seat. My philosophy is if we are only provided seats in the back of the bus, then we must build our own buses! Society and its economic system have gone out of its way to provide us with the engine, wheels, tires, and all the other necessary materials to do just that.

I would like to thank you all for reading and supporting this work. Please continue to support my efforts to spread these ideas to the world by following me and purchasing more of my products. This work has provided you with enough foundational knowledge to send you and your sphere of influence on a different path. A better path. A path that provides you with the power to make your life whatever you want it to be. I am counting on you to stay the course no matter what. You and the great things you accomplish will be my inspiration. No matter what, always remember to adhere to these key principles.

<u>How Losers Win</u>

1. Always embrace your inner loser with pride and glee.

2. Unplug yourself from the matrix and be persistent in

your resistance to its constant pull on your psyche.

3. Do the work to find out who you truly are and continue to revisit yourself so that you never become lost again.

4. Always make it a point to mind your own business.

5. Incorporate your businesses and use business credit as a strategic platform to always be economically free.

I look forward to experiencing many of your wonderful works in the future!